I0142538

The Essentials

Everything Women Need to Know to
Make It as a Network Marketer

Copyright © 2020 by Kacie Vaudrey

All rights reserved. No part of this book may be reproduced in any form or by any means—electronic, mechanical, photocopying, or scanning—without written permission from the author except by reviewers who may quote.

Kacie Vaudrey LLC
www.KacieVaudrey.com

Publisher's Cataloging-In-Publication Data
Names: Vaudrey, Kacie, author.
Title: The essentials : everything women need to know to make it as a
    network marketer / Kacie Vaudrey.
Description: [Park City, Utah] : Kacie Vaudrey LLC, [2019]
Identifiers: ISBN 9781734082739 (paperback) | ISBN 9781734082746
(ebook)
Subjects: LCSH: Multilevel marketing. | Women in marketing.
Classification: LCC HF5415.126 .V38 2019 (print) | LCC HF5415.126
(ebook)
    | DDC 658.84—dc23

Printed in the United States of America

This publication is designed to provide accurate and authoritative information with regard to the subject matter covered. It is sold with the understanding that neither the author nor the publisher is engaged in rendering legal, accounting, or other professional advice. If legal advice or other expert assistance is required, the services of a competent professional person should be sought.

To all the amazing female network marketers who took a chance on this industry, show up every day, follow their dreams, and live a next-level life

PRAISE

"Kacie Vaudrey is a wealth of knowledge in the field of network marketing! She is a trusted friend and a gifted mentor. I am forever thankful for her willingness to guide and help!"

—Sara Janssen, Speaker, Business Coach, Blogger, Founder and CEO of TribeLife and www.nestinggypsy.com

"Anyone, especially women, who are considering network marketing as a way to regain autonomy in their lives and freedom and flexibility in their money-making needs to read The Essentials! *If you are scared of sales, of being pushy, or of any of the other million lies we tell ourselves when our fear rises up but so badly want to be your own boss, do yourself a favor and let Kacie Vaudrey be your mentor and guide. Kacie is one of the most genuine, real, down-to-earth women I have had the privilege of knowing. Perhaps it's her perspective and life experiences, but you can tell that she truly knows that life is a gift and that time is our most precious resource. Kacie is kind, so smart, and, most importantly, truly heart-led about her work. To watch her dedication to both her business and her oiling community has been an honor. To be able to consider her a peer and a friend is such a tremendous blessing."*

—Li Fryling, BFA, B.Ed., CEO of North Star Essentials

"I'm excited for the refreshing take on integrity that The Essentials is for the network marketing business. Kacie Vaudrey is the perfect person to write this book. She is the epitome of a wise and humble leader. She is among the top 1 percent in the world with her achievements. Even with what she has accomplished, Kacie totally comes across as the girl next door. She's available for strategy, and she's available as a friend. Kacie has a lot of experience and success to stand on. Yet there's no pretense. She has a comfortable demeanor that makes everything she says fall on soft ears."

—Dana Moore, Founder and CEO of Moore Essentials, LLC &
Live Naturally Tools, Inc.

"I am so excited about The Essentials and the knowledge and guidance Kacie Vaudrey is bringing to so many other women just like me. Kacie was the angel who fell into my life at a time when I didn't even realize I needed her. Network marketing was so foreign to me. Kacie, from states away, took me under her wing. Not knowing me at all, she helped me grow an incredible business. She's been a friend and mentor. She's guided me, nurtured me, and given me tough love when needed. She's been exactly what I need and what other people need when trying to grow this business. Kacie has integrity. She's generous. She's willing to give anything to anyone to watch them reach their goals and fulfill their dreams. She is so passionate about making sure people gain time freedom and happiness—whatever that looks like."

—Melissa Vallelunga, RN, MSN, WHNP, Owner of
Living Essentially, LLC

"Kacie Vaudrey is one of the most genuine people I know with a HUGE heart! I am so fortunate to learn from her wealth of knowledge on how to build this business effectively. One of my favorite things is to see women empowering women, and Kacie does this in such a simple and authentic way."

—Jessica Iddings, Founder and CEO of Simply Essential, LLC &
Type 1 Natural Mama

"If you are ever having any feelings of doubt around direct sales or in your ability to succeed in this booming industry, I highly recommend you take in and apply Kacie Vaudrey's seasoned and thoughtful words. Kacie has played an integral role in my business and personal growth journey through her heart-led mentorship and in her ability to demystify the untruths around network marketing. In doing so, Kacie offered me a hand to rise above my fears and self-doubt, empowering me to take my first steps into the beauty of the unknown. This is a movement that is proving to be one of the best decisions of my professional career. Have no doubt that Kacie will also lead you authentically with integrity, truth, and love down the path to the best possible version of you and your business."

—Mary Van Laarhoven, PharmD, RYT,
President of Pain to Peace, Inc.

CONTENTS

CHAPTER 1

THE BEST GIG ON THE FACE OF THE EARTH

Remember the first time a friend of yours told you about A Wonderful Opportunity? Remember The Business Plan slideshow with all those perfect glossy photos? And the pitch. Don't forget how she sold you The Dream . . .

"If you bring just three people into this business, you can earn millions of dollars, take ten vacations a year, build your dream home in your dream neighborhood, and own a freaking yacht . . . all while working only five hours a week. *That* is what it means to be successful."

Of course you remember. Feels like yesterday, doesn't it? Once you saw how *easy* this business could be, you couldn't un-see the passive income flowing into your checking account every week. Then you told people. Your family, your girlfriends, your coworkers. And what did they all say when they found out you'd joined—*gasp*—a multilevel marketing company?

"Don't do it."

"Waste of time."

"No thanks. Not interested."

"Pyramid scheme. Can you get your money back?"

"Only 1 percent of MLMers make it. You really think you're going to be one of them?"

You sure thought so. For a while, the dream lived on. You bought all the personal development books, listened to company success stories, and attended functions all across the country to meet other future millionaires. You've been *loving* this industry. Everything about it. The relationships you've built and the mentoring you've received fill your heart. This is the best business in the world.

Except for one little thing. Sales. You haven't been making them. At least, not as many as you need to make a down payment on that yacht. No matter how motivated you are or how hard you work, The Dream is always out of reach.

When you first heard about network marketing, you were sold two completely different sets of expectations. The first was success beyond your wildest dreams. The second was failure straight out of your worst nightmare. Going forward, you have two possible futures in this industry. You'll either be able to take summers off to backpack the Andes, or you'll work thirty hours a week on top of a full-time job to make an extra hundred bucks a week. Only that hallowed 1 percent get to climb up to Machu Picchu—the other 99 percent get to climb out of credit card debt. I'm here to tell you that's just not the case.

WHAT NETWORKING MARKETING IS REALLY ABOUT

Popular expectations about network marketing are frightening because they're *so* far from the truth. You're not likely to live out *either* of the futures above. Reality is somewhere in the middle. A true happy medium. As for that 1 percent success category? One percent of people in our industry become multilevel multi*millionaires*. Way more than that build successful businesses that support their ideal lifestyle. Take my family. We don't own a fleet of yachts, but we can pay our bills, fund our dreams, and have plenty left over to take a vacation and donate to our favorite charity.

Best of all, we get a wonderful little thing I like to call schedule manipulation. We can work our business around our lives, not the other way around like every other profession. Why wouldn't you want this lifestyle? To have the flexibility to go hang out with your kiddos in the middle of the afternoon on a Monday? Or quit work early and have a late lunch with your girlfriends? Just last week, my hairdresser texted me when she had a cancellation. *Any chance you could come two hours earlier at noon?* I didn't have to check with my boss, cancel any meetings, or get a coworker to cover for me. When she saw my reply, I'd already gone to her website and booked the appointment. One more reason I love owning a business.

Now, don't get me wrong. If I want to be an inspirational coach and an industry leader, guess what? I have to show up. When my phone blows up with texts and phone calls, I have to make time to answer. But it's on *my* schedule. I'm not tied to my phone twenty-four seven like other women entrepreneurs. You wouldn't want to be reading this book if that were the case! *If I wait more than five minutes to respond to this prospect, I might lose the sale.* No, that's definitely not me. This business has taught me to respect my time and set boundaries so I don't lose that feeling of control or miss out on the things that matter most. It's not *complete* time freedom, but it's the next best thing. Same with financial freedom. We've never hired live-in nannies, but we do have fully funded retirement accounts for ourselves and college savings for the kids. And house cleaners. Can't forget those. I'll never give up my cleaners. Every two weeks the house is spotless, and I can do my happy dance. Seems reasonable, right?

When I started my business, you know what my goal was? *If I can do this for two years and work my way up to $5,000 a month, I'll have complete success.* If I'd let industry expectations become *my* expectations, I never would've taken the leap. Everyone should have a different idea of what MLM success looks like for their situation. You don't have to earn $20,000 a month. Maybe an extra $500 a month would transform your personal finances, and that's all you have time for right now. If that's your goal, this industry can give it to you. *You* own your big picture, not the person selling you The Dream.

"Oh, so you're in a pyramid scheme. SCAM!" clueless people still tell me.

I laugh. Then I ask what they do.

Here's the reality that no one can deny. In a traditional job, you don't get to control how much you earn, who you work with, when you have to show up, or how much impact you have on the masses. Unless you're the CEO, you're always working for someone else with little to no true skin in the game. This business gives you control over all of that. Your performance determines your results. If you fail, it's on you.

I used to long for that kind of control over my destiny. When I was a college professor, I was never going to earn more than $2,400 a month. For eight years, I got zero raises. To increase my salary, I would've had to take on more classes. Generally speaking, four courses was the maximum load. Most adjunct faculty stuck with two or three. I can see why. I taught four courses every semester, and I was exhausted every evening. Yet no matter how hard I worked, I didn't lift my paycheck a dime. Sure, a university job gave me status. Prestige. People thought I had it all. But when the opportunity presented itself, I gave it all up for the best gig on the face of the earth— multilevel marketing.

Like many women who consider this business, I was afraid of failing and becoming a statistic. I kept my little secret business buried in my heart and threw away the key. For eighteen months, I contemplated how I would share with friends and family my desire to change careers and become the CEO of my own business. I'm not talking a side gig—I'm talking a full-time career. A no-turning-back kind of business. What would they think? That Kacie went off the deep end? What about all those years of college? Health insurance? Job security? What did I know about sales? Blah, blah, blah. Yet I knew in my heart I was making the right choice. Not for them—for *me*. I chose the right company, followed the right system, and dove in headfirst. And still to this day, when I stop and think about how it all came out, it makes me smile.

So, after nearly two years of running my business in secret, it was time to come clean. Over dinner with my parents and their friends, the news came out a little something like this.

"Hey, Dad? So . . . I have some money saved up. I've also got some money in my 401(k)," I said as I took a huge bite of steak. I think I was secretly hoping to choke to avoid any kind of conversation past this point. "How would you recommend I invest?"

Without blinking, he and his investor buddy went on about all the smart ways to make my money work for me and prepare for my future—investment opportunities I was clueless about.

"OK." I nodded. "Thanks. I was asking because I'm not at the university anymore. I'm saving way more than I ever have."

In walked my mom.

"You *what*?! You lost your job? Kacie—"

"*Mom*," I breathed, "I quit the university so I could join a network marketing company full-time." You should've seen their faces. "You know how much I've made over the last twelve months?" My big smile made me look like a crazy person. What did I care? This was my moment. "I've earned triple what I was making at the university."

"What?" Mom exchanged a glance with Dad. "You're . . . you're joking, right?"

"No, Mom. That's what network marketing has allowed me to do for my family. And get this—by the end of next year, I expect to *double* the size of my business."

Then she smiled. And I realized that, although the questions I'd been dreading were probably valid, they didn't matter. I'd officially broken the stigma around network marketing for myself and for my family. All because I created *my* success story based on *my* goal. *I've made it.*

What about you? How do you become one of those people who "makes it"? How do you even know if this is the right thing for you? Simple. This business can be for anyone. It can be for the person who wants to help impoverished countries drill wells and build schools. It could be for someone who wants to travel the world while they work. It could be for somebody who wants to disrupt our health care system. It could be for somebody who wants to help other women find the same level of success they have. It could be for somebody who wants to get out of the house and spend more time with girlfriends. It could be for somebody who wants to find their voice and put themselves out there. It could be for somebody who wants to be in charge of their paycheck. And it could be for someone who wants to help people in need who cross their path.

I hope one thing is clear to you. You don't have to pick and choose what you get out of networking marketing—you *can* have it all. You *can* be successful while chasing your kids around. You *can* make a difference in the world without giving up those little things that just make you happy. And you *can* be an amazing wife and mother while running a successful business from home. That's what makes multilevel marketing the ideal business model. It works so well with our everyday lives (and responsibilities) as women. No other career offers this flexibility.

Now, that doesn't mean we get to spend every minute with loved ones. I travel on business. And that mom guilt I feel when I pull out of the driveway is *normal*. You know what I'm talking about. As women, when we achieve success, our gut tells us to feel guilty because we left the kids at home and aren't spending more time with them. Our kids won't remember that we were out building our business and providing for our family. What will they remember? I've always wanted my kids to remember that Mom was there for them when they needed me. That's why, when I started my business, I made a pact with myself. *No matter what, if my kids need me, I will stop what I'm doing. Even if I'm traveling, I'll get on the phone with them or open up*

Skype. Even if I'm on a work call, I'll reschedule and hang up. I will *be present with them in that moment. I* will *be there when they need me.* Because of network marketing, I've kept that pact. I can't think of any other job where I could have done that. And all the while, residual income flows straight into my bank account.

As my kids have gotten older, I've included them in goal-setting sessions along with my husband, Mike, so they understand why we do what we do. We talk about what we want as a family and what it will take to get there.

"We chose this lifestyle as a family," I remind everyone. "Together, we all have to make some compromises. But they *will* be worth it." And they always are.

Over 110,000 women have come into my business to experience this same lifestyle on their terms. Deep down, we all desire a feminine approach to business that no one else has given us. We want the relationships. The community. The coaching. We want someone cheering us on. Sometimes that connection is all we need to reach our goals. I believe we can build a business from a genuine place. You don't lose your identity. Your identity just gets better. You up-level everything about yourself. You get to influence more people. You get to play more. You get to participate in more women's lives. You get to leverage your innate empathy. As women, we're put on this earth to give, to nurture, and to love. When one woman succeeds, we *all* succeed. That's community. That's empowerment. That's network marketing.

There's something powerful about having something become yours. Not in a selfish way. When you join this business, it becomes a part of who you are. Too many women bust their butts to live up to societal norms and external expectations. We strive to be the woman, wife, and mother who pleases everyone but ourselves. But when we have something that's all our own, and we get to choose how much money we make, where we spend our time, and who we spend it with, we show up as our best self in every area of life. Honestly, nothing is sexier than somebody who owns their destiny—and knows it.

No wonder so many women try direct sales. By 2020, half the population will work from home.[1] Many for a home-based business like mine. Already, three-quarters of direct marketers are women.[2] In years gone by, no girl ever said, "I want to be a saleswoman when I grow up." But now, when you find the right direct sales company, you don't have to check your personality at the door. You can be yourself. You can bring your feminine side. You can help other people while forming a fulfilling community of women from diverse backgrounds. Traditionally, we've found a community in church or through shared activities like yoga class or a children's book club. The connection you get in network marketing is different. It's *enticing*. In direct sales, we have skin in the game. We're leading teams. We're working with like-minded women on a similar mission, whether that's improving our own health, helping people lose weight, or making people feel more beautiful. When you're building true community, you don't have to be aggressive, pitch products to friends from high school, and get yourself blocked on social media. I've had enough of those people who poison our industry. I don't need them in my life, and you don't need them in yours. You're a giver, not a taker. So let your business reflect who you are. I remember when I committed to building a business eight years ago, I got my first few "OMG THANK YOU" texts from my customers. I'd get messages at two o'clock in the morning because a child no longer had a fever or a mom was no longer suffering from anxiety.

Are you feeling the magic? The power of this industry? It's the one place where you can enjoy the success you desire—and deserve. It's just too dang good. So now that you know what network marketing is all about, I want to give you a simple system to build the business *you* want to build. The essential parts of this system to build your business include:

- Choosing the right business (and mentor) to set you up for success

- Earning your first $1,000 while you're still in a nine-to-five

- Setting goals and structuring your life so you achieve them

- Scheduling money-making activities so you never waste a day

- Building relationships with customers and team members

- Staying true to your message in your marketing so people engage

- Keeping your motivation up when sales slow (and they always do)

No fluff, no hype—just the essentials you need to build a multimillion-dollar network marketing business, if you so desire. I'll help you surround yourself with good people who believe in the product as much as you do, and together, you'll blow up your industry.

CHAPTER 2

BEFORE YOU START (OR QUIT)

Do you know what frustrates me most about this business? I meet so many women who dive into network marketing for all the wrong reasons. They buy into the yacht vision, but when a boat doesn't fall into their lap, they say whatever it takes to move product. What about authenticity? Too inconvenient. Reality catches up quick. They lose all their friends. They don't get approved for that sixth credit card. Or worse, they lose everything when a class-action lawsuit comes calling (yes, that happens).

You know what else is frustrating? Women who leave direct sales for all the wrong reasons. For some reason, when many women in network marketing get thrown to the ground once, they throw up their arms and quit. They second-guess themselves all the time. *What credibility do I have? How can I ever* *be successful? Why do I deserve to dream about making $10,000 or even $20,000 a month?* They just wanted to prove their killjoy in-laws wrong. The all-expenses-paid Hawaii vacations? Those were a bonus. But that humble vision never materialized. Unsold product clutters every corner and cabinet of their house. *Why am I spending $2,000 a month to earn a few hundred?* So they stop attending the conferences. They let upline calls go to voice mail. And whatever meager residual income they've built up dwindles down to nothing over the next few months. They never officially "quit," but they delete the company name from all social media bios and email signatures. Their professional networking profile headline goes from "Independent Consultant" to "Seeking New Opportunities."

I wish I got to these women before it was too late. I would've asked them the one question that turns any direct sales business around. The question that answers all other questions. The one I'm about to ask you. Leave this unanswered when you join an MLM (or worse, don't think to ask it) and you'll fumble your way into debt and ruin your reputation. If you're already in business, you'll quit prematurely.

So what's the question?

What outcome do I want from networking marketing that I don't already have?

I choose these words for a reason. I'm not asking you, "Hey, what do you want out of this MLM thing anyway?" I want to know what *outcome* you desire that *you don't yet have*. And be specific. Outcomes are not the same as goals. A goal is like a car.

An outcome is like the BMW convertible where the sexiest moments of your marriage happen as you're parked atop a seaside cliff under a full moon. Outcomes are so vivid they make your whole body tingle when you think about them. Some goals are so vague they don't include a plan to achieve them.

The two types of women I mentioned on the last page have goals. But they have no clue what outcomes they're after. Don't get me wrong—I see nothing wrong with owning a boat or telling off your condescending family. But we get into MLM (or get out of it) for all the wrong reasons when we don't make this business personally fulfilling. That picture of a yacht someone showed you? Probably not what you, personally, daydream about. Getting sweet revenge because you're rolling in piles of cash? Personal maybe, but not fulfilling.

What's led me to network marketing success is clarity on the outcomes I want. I can't get these results anywhere else. I left my nine-to-five at the university to dive into this business full-time for three reasons. First, I wanted to take care of my health. I believe that the stress of my old life contributed in part to my cancer. Second, I hated working my butt off yet holding no control over my income. I knew that if I committed to my own business, I would create financial freedom and provide my kids the lifestyle they deserve. Third, I wanted flexibility in my schedule. That's the hardest thing about a nine-to-five job— people rely on you to show up for work every single day. As a professor, I had twenty-four students expecting me to be there. You don't get a sub in college. I hated that commitment. I couldn't take time off, not even when one of my kids had to stay home sick (thank goodness for grandparents and friends). The *only* opportunity to produce these three personal outcomes was (and still is) networking marketing. For me, these three intended outcomes are personal, fulfilling, and, best of all, possible. After all, they came to pass not even two years into my business.

It's not too late to figure out what outcomes you desire that you don't have yet. I'm here to help you look before you leap, whatever your situation. It doesn't matter if you want to quit your nine-to-five or get back to work after being a stay-at-home mom. Anytime you want to make a shift, you need to feel good about it before you make the change. Without a clear outcome in your heart, you'll feel uneasy. Unsettled. Unprepared. You'll take a leap with the wrong intention—with a goal that, deep down, doesn't matter that much to you.

What outcome do I want from networking marketing that I don't already have? It's harder to answer than you'd think, isn't it? So how do you dig deep enough to find the true outcomes your heart desires? Start by getting off your butt, grabbing your journal and a pen (or a notepad app on your phone), and asking yourself these questions:

- What are you looking for in life?
- Why are you seeking change?
- Why do you want a new career?
- How do you visualize MLM working in your life?
- What will your schedule look like when you take on this new opportunity?

- What are you willing to commit to?

- What are you willing to give up to make this change?

- What value is this going to add to you, to your family, to your finances, to your health?

When you've answered these questions, look at your notes. Can you identify the outcomes you want? It helps to use the words "so that." As in, "I'm willing to commit to ten hours a week now *so that* I can earn my first thousand dollars a month *so that* we can pay off the mortgage early *so that* we can save for a motor home *so that* we can take road trips when we retire *so that* we can live happy and well in our golden years."

See how this works, sister? I want you to start with the end in mind. When you know your ultimate outcome, you'll feel confident to talk to your family and friends about your business. You'll enjoy the flexibility to grow your business while still working a day job. You'll want to get up in the morning and work. And you'll develop the wisdom to choose the right mentor to rocket you to the next level.

HOW TO TELL FAMILY AND FRIENDS SO THEY DON'T FREAK OUT

In a recent social media group post, I asked my team, "What would it be like if we lived in a perfect world where no one judged network marketing? What if working in this industry was as prestigious as teaching at a university?"

A girl can dream, right? It's hard to find the confidence to dive into this industry headfirst. When I graduated high school, went on to college, and earned a double bachelor's degree and a master's, my parents were so proud of me. As a college professor, I loved telling people what I did for a living. I'm not going to lie. When I started selling oils, it was hard to choke out the words.

"Well, I joined an MLM . . ."

Going from wearing my job title on my sleeve to dodging the dreaded "What do you do?" question at parties was a major shift. It's challenging to find the confidence to dive into that discomfort. Yet that's what makes all the difference in how people perceive you.

As a society, we push people to decide on a career they want to stay in for a lifetime. We let other people's vision for the ideal life dictate how we roll. Unfortunately, network marketing isn't a career choice parents recommend to their kids. If our families talked about direct sales as a serious career choice like law or medicine, this industry would never have a stigma.

When we talk about direct sales without knowing the outcome we want, we go into freak-out mode. *What will people think? What will they say? Who will judge me?* In my case, I knew what outcomes I wanted, so no matter what flack I got (and I got my share), I knew it'd be worth it. I wanted something more enticing than a career people respected. That job couldn't give me everything I desired for my family. When I found this opportunity, this business became so much more than a career. It became this passion around empowering other people to be leaders, to raise up fellow women, to reach our full potential. I can't think of a better place for me than this industry. I'm grateful I broke free from other people's expectations. You can, too.

This industry would be most people's sweet spot if they allowed themselves to commit. It provides the most time freedom, schedule freedom, and financial freedom of any career choice I've found. The beauty of network marketing is we have time when things come up. If my kiddos are sick, I want to be able to take the day off. I don't want to have to call my boss, ask if someone can cover for me, and take a vacation day. Or what if I just don't feel like working that day? Because we all have those days when we just don't want to. What if you *didn't* have to drag yourself off the sofa, down a pot of coffee, and trudge into the office? What if you could just take a day for yourself? Who wouldn't want that?

If life were always that easy, we wouldn't have to be brave. We wouldn't have to face the stigma head-on. People will judge you anyway. When they do, you have two choices. You can walk away, let their words haunt you, and give up too soon. Or you can know your outcomes and wow people, shutting them up where they stand (if mouths hang open, that's a plus).

Let me teach you choice number two. When you talk to family and friends about your networking marketing business, describe what you do as sales or referral marketing. Most people get that. Direct sales is no different from recommending a good hair salon to a girlfriend, referring your dad to a trustworthy car dealership, or sharing a tasty recipe on social media. When we love something or something works well for us, we want to share it with everyone. Look at this industry as an opportunity to share a product you love without having a middleman (or woman) to sell it.

For example, I've had a version of this conversation many times:

"So what's new, Kacie? Still teaching?"

"Actually, I left the college. I own a home-based essential oils business."

"You mean like multilevel marketing? A pyramid scheme? Kacie, those are scams. Pretty sure they're, like, illegal. People lose *so* much money."

"Actually, those are all common misconceptions about this business. It's true that many people who try network marketing give us a bad rap. Do you know where they go wrong?"

"Uh . . . no?"

"They're not passionate about what they sell, so they come across cheesy and salesy. What I do is completely different. I'm on a mission to educate people about essential oils so they can take their health care into their own hands. Plus, I still get to teach. And I help thousands of women all over the country to build their own successful business while enjoying more time with their kiddos than ever before."

"Oh . . . well. Still, that business is risky. Why don't you get a reliable job with a steady paycheck and good benefits? Your children—"

"Actually, my kids are a big part of why I started my business. Now that I get to control my own schedule, I'm available whenever they need me. And I can afford to give them things that were *way* outside my budget when I was a professor. Not to mention I have so much less stress because I take care of *me*. Wouldn't you agree that providing for my family and taking care of my health should be my top priority?"

"Oh, of course. Well, sounds like you've really got things together. What's your company again?"

Perceptions shift fast when you speak with confidence. The way to get that confidence is to know your outcomes. This is *your* dream. This is *your* life. If you still don't quite have your confidence up, I can help. In the space provided below, prepare your loving comeback in advance. When someone you know or love brings up direct sales stigma, you'll feel ready to stand up for yourself. Build on your conviction today, stand up tall tomorrow.

How has your product changed your life?

_____

_____

_____

_____

_____

_____

_____

Name the top three ways you use your product.

_____

_____

_____

_____

_____

_____

_____

Who do you know that needs your product?

_____

_____

_____

_____

_____

_____

_____

_____

Nowadays, no one ever gets away with judging me. I'm so passionate about this industry and what it can offer to the masses, most don't dare challenge me. Anytime I catch someone insulting this industry, I reply, "You're right. I *hate* having the opportunity to be in charge of my own paycheck, own my time, and create a multimillion-dollar business. It's the *worst*. My kids *hate* having an entrepreneur as a mom."

Not going to lie—it feels good. Why should you have to justify your career? You shouldn't. That said, sarcasm isn't always a smart play. If you're still facing skepticism after sharing what MLM has done for you, move on to a magic little word. What do the best salespeople in any industry do to convert skeptics into evangelists? Simple—*free*. That's what worked on my parents after they found out I'd left the university to build up my business.

I've always been a hippie to my parents. From the time I was eighteen years old, I've been using essential oils, eating organic, and worrying about the planet. So starting my business wasn't a total shock. But they weren't receptive about MLM or essential oils. They lacked experience and knowledge. Not their fault. Sales is about identifying and solving a pain spot with minimal to no chance for error.

To soften my parents, I gave my dad a free lavender essential oil roller bottle to help him sleep. I chose something I knew would provide quick results without confusing directions. My parents' trust lies in Western medicine, which I totally get. My only goal was to get Dad to be open to trying the product. He loved it. Now, I have my parents using essential oil diffusers.

They're sharing them with every single one of their friends. My mom calls me several times a month to ask my advice on relieving aches and pains. It may take your family and friends years to embrace your new business, lifestyle, and priorities. And that's OK. Love them where they're at, and keep sharing the free goods.

What if tension at home isn't about the product, though? What if it's about the money? For most women, success is scary. What happens to friendships when you can afford to take vacations they can't? What happens to your spouse when you make more money than they do? Time and time again, I have to remind women it's OK to be successful. And too often, they reply, "Kacie, I can't be too successful because it threatens the people around me . . . especially my husband."

I don't care what year it is or how progressive you are. A weird dynamic occurs when a woman earns more money than her partner. Same with your family and friends. They don't want to be part of your life anymore. Your success threatens them. They feel guilty. After guilt comes bitterness.

If I could do it all again, would I change anything? Would I trade my success for relationships that ended *because* of my success? No *freaking way*. I'm so much happier. Give yourself grace and allow yourself to choose what fits into your picture. Feel proud of whatever it is you want—*you deserve it*. That's real gratitude. Celebrate everything you have. Take my daughter. When she competes in a ski event and places well, she doesn't apologize. She doesn't concede her place. She won, and she wears it with pride. She deserves the praise, and let me tell you, she enjoys it. So should you, sister.

I remember the first month I earned more money than Mike. I was a little terrified. This wasn't customary in my world. Mike surprised me. "Oh my gosh, babe, you totally blew my paycheck out of the water! Let's celebrate."

This is a true partnership. We're in the sweet spot. It doesn't matter if I earn more money or he does; it's *our* money. We're using it to live our best life as a family. Too often that's not the case. Let's say a new builder gets high on adrenaline because our products can change someone's life. Maybe her newest customer texts her saying, "Oh my gosh. You just made my child sleep through the night. You're a miracle worker." Then my superstar goes home and tells her husband the good news.

"This woman thanked *me*." She can barely contain her excitement. "I never knew how fulfilling it was to help people *and* get paid for it. Look how much I earned this month. If I keep enrolling customers, we'll have enough saved to take the kids to Disneyland next summer."

"Whoa, honey. You need to reel it in," hubby says. "I don't know if expanding is such a great idea. Look at the house. The sink's overflowing with dishes. This is my last clean shirt. I had to take the kids out for dinner twice this week. *Twice*."

"But you said—"

"Now, I don't mind pitching in with some chores, but I work, you know. Full-time. A real job. I don't have it in me to be Dad and Mom in this family. Plus, my paycheck is guaranteed.

Don't you have to go out and find people to sell this stuff? You never know if you're going to get people to buy, right?"

"Well, no, but—"

"Don't you want to come back home and do the stay-at-home-mom thing? The kids and I miss having you around more."

Just like that, my superstar's spirit falls. Her husband feels threatened. Instead of celebrating her, he gets jealous. He hates change. He doesn't offer the support his wife deserves. Add a side of mom guilt and I'll count it a miracle if my team member doesn't quit direct sales altogether.

"I want to keep building my business, but I don't have any support at home." If I had a dollar—no, a *dime* for every time a woman said that to me, I wouldn't need this industry to be financially secure.

What if that's your story? Try talking it out with your partner like rational people. Deal with facts first, emotions second. Fact one: more money for the family is a *good* thing. Fact two: it doesn't matter who brings in more money as long as the family's needs get met. Once you agree on these facts, discuss the emotions you both have around them. Consider a professional counselor or therapist to help you sort through those feelings.

HOW TO OWN YOUR DECISION TO JOIN AN MLM

When we make the choice to follow our own path and stop bearing the weight of what other people think, that's when we're able to achieve our vision for our ideal life. I'm so grateful

I broke free from that cycle. It took me a while to get there. If that's where you are, let me encourage you. Let's see this business as a nonnegotiable. I'll explain.

When I was diagnosed with breast cancer, I found out they couldn't hold my position at the college while I underwent treatment. So I either had to find another job (one that would be OK with extended absences) or make a major career shift. I was already head over heels for the product, but I'd struggled with the stigma around shifting from teaching to direct sales. Then I realized something—*it wasn't negotiable.* I needed to work, I couldn't continue at the college, and this opportunity offered the flexibility I required.

These practical reasons pushed me over the edge of my indecision and allowed me to view the opportunity in a new light. I took the plunge. Every day I'm grateful that I did. At the end of the day, you and only you know what's best for you. You're the only one who can choose the right path, because you're the only one who can follow it. Even the most well-meaning friends and family members can't make decisions for you. If and when you live an extraordinary life, big things happen. I can't imagine taking the career path other people wanted for me. Today, I'm superconfident in everything I do. My kids love this industry. They already know they want to be entrepreneurs. They'll probably never work for somebody else. Who would want to give up the lifestyle that business ownership provides? My kids understand (and I hope you do, too) that this career choice *is* acceptable.

I want to share possibly the best advice I've ever gotten. It was from my cancer doctor during my four-week post-op appointment. She looked up from my paperwork and said, "Kacie, it's time to go and start living your life." Although her comment didn't directly correlate with the business, I carry this message with me day to day. That was my permission to break free.

Now I want to offer you the same piece of advice. If we were hanging out on my front porch or chatting on the phone, I would tell you to own what you do once and for all. If you want to seize the network marketing opportunity and stay at home with the kids or keep pursuing your high-power career while building a business on the side, go for it.

Have you ever seen those blinders they put on horses to keep them focused? Owning your path is your equivalent to horse blinders. That means not allowing yourself to get distracted by how other people are doing things. You and your family have determined a vision, created goals, and put together what it will take to get there. If it's working for you, that's enough. Turn a deaf ear to the judgments that may surround it. Regardless of what people around us do, we are in control of our own destinies. We live in exciting times. Please don't let stigma keep you from living the life that makes sense for you and your family. Because when you're passionate about something, it's selfish *not* to go for it. The world needs what you have to offer, so don't hide your light for the sake of social pressures. Share what you know to be true, and follow your dreams without justification. I can't wait to see where they take you.

HOW TO DO MLM AND A NINE-TO-FIVE WITHOUT GETTING FIRED

Let me set something straight. I don't view a nine-to-five as a horrible way to live your life. Sometimes I'm a little envious of people who get to check out as soon as the clock reaches five. I'm always thinking about work. If you're in a nine-to-five job where you get to inspire people (and feel inspired yourself), don't put in your two weeks' notice yet. Even if you can't climb the ladder any higher, keep that steady paycheck while you move your business forward. Whether you're a teacher, a coal miner, or a 7-Eleven cashier, you don't have to quit your job to make your first thousand dollars as a network marketer. Building your business the organic way is the best way to build this business—and talk about your products with coworkers without being annoying.

It all comes down to listening to people's needs. People complain about the same things all the time. Health. Finances. Spiritual well-being. Emotional well-being. Their current relationship status. Network marketing is truly the all-encompassing solution. It doesn't matter what you're selling as long as you love the product. True community is this industry's natural outcome. When you listen to people's needs and address them, you simply *can't* be anything but a blessing. Where people fail in building this business is insincerity. If you're in it for the right reasons, you get the right result.

Remember your desired outcomes? The result you're working toward allows you to build your business on *your* terms. That means you *don't* have to spam your coworkers or quit your day job. Maybe that's what the couple in your upline did. But their story isn't yours. Before you take the leap, make sure everything is in alignment. That means your heart, your health, your finances, your mental stability, your family. If everything is in place, ready for you to make this change, you won't cause yourself more stress and heartache. After all, making this decision should be fun. So take the time to map it out. Grab that pen again. Ask yourself:

- What is your career shift going to look like?

- How much do you need to make to achieve your desired outcomes?

- How soon can you reach that point and leave your nine-to-five?

- What can you do right now that gets you one day closer to your last at that job?

While you're going about daily life (even at your nine-to-five), be on the lookout for other like-minded people to join your circle of influence. Naturally, the faculty I ran around with at the university were health-conscious. Guess who my first customers were?

So again, don't quit your nine-to-five tomorrow. Your current job is an excellent place to network and share with those who already know and trust you. I officially started my business while working forty hours a week on campus and spending another ten hours grading papers. I shied away from calling my products a business. I referred to it as my mission or my obligation. That sounds strong, but for me, that's what it was. I had a career. I didn't want another job or responsibility.

Yet I had a mission in my heart to get these oils into every person's home. I felt an obligation to share everything I knew. So I learned how to work the business around what I was already doing. If I was having a girls' night, I brought product. If I was singing songs with my kiddos at KinderMusik, I brought oils. If I was chatting with colleagues about our income, I was sharing the business opportunity. I grew my business the organic way because it was part of my lifestyle. Use your current job as a place to network and engage with others about what you're up to.

Just because I had my own insecurities and fears around calling my business a job doesn't mean I didn't treat it like a job. I was not about to put one toe in and never leap. I had to work the business around my current lifestyle with as little disruption as possible. My own personal balance. For you, that may mean that you keep your job for a few more months. Or years. Or even longer. And that's OK. Network marketing is the industry for anyone who wants a little more flexibility in life. If you love your job but want a little extra money to splurge on yourself because you deserve it, this industry is perfect for you. And if you want to fire your boss yesterday, you've come to the right space. Whatever your story up to this point, starting a network marketing business means the best is yet to come.

HOW TO FIND THE RIGHT COACHING: A $100,000 LESSON

Why would someone even think they need a coach? When we start a network marketing business, we want all the answers all at once. We don't care who the solutions come from. So we hire coaches. Lots of coaches. I honestly thought hiring a coach would jump-start my business, solve my problems, and make me a better leader. Although I feel that coaches add value to the industry, it's crucial that we work with the right people.

I've spent over $100,000 on personal coaching for my business, so let me give you a few pieces of advice when looking for the right mentor. Find out what you can get for free before you shell out a ton of cash. Sometimes we get so caught up buying coaching programs. *But it's only $197. I've got to do it. It's going to be amazing.* Too often that membership causes financial strain. Even worse, we pay all this money yet don't have the time to commit to it. Or if we do commit, we find out the coach isn't the right person for us.

For most business builders, it makes sense to start with the training your company is offering. If you start there and do the activities that top leaders recommend, you will find success. Others are like me—you want to go deeper and learn every money-making secret out there. Before you go all in on any business coach or training program outside your company, watch as many free videos and webinars as you can. See what you love about their presentation and what you could do without. The more material you can watch from different experts, the better chance you have to make sure someone is a good fit before you invest any money.

The one coach I want you to avoid is the one who assigns you distractions. For example, if your coach prioritizes vision boards but you've already created one with complete clarity, that person is probably not a good fit. People spend thousands and thousands of dollars going through activities and programs when all they needed to do was start working. If you want to distract yourself from doing what you know you should do to hit your goal, go get coaching from the wrong person. They'll tell you to peruse social media all day, messaging random people with links to your products. Let me save you time and money. That approach never works. If your coach doesn't hold you accountable to money-making activities, then friend, you're with the wrong coach.

If that's who *not* to choose, which coach *should* you choose? Go back to your desired outcomes. This is where a lot of MLM newbies go wrong. If your vision board shows off dreams your upline gave you, you'll never find the right coach to help you make it. If you don't know what you want, how can someone else help you get it? When you're super clear on the outcome you're working toward, the right coach is your GPS, giving you the best route to arrive at your destination. Here are some great questions to think about (and ask) so you can find the right mentor for the right season of your business:

- What training is your current company offering?

- Where do you need the most help?

- What have you found useful in the desired area for free? What's still missing?

- What is this coach's multilevel marketing experience? Do you want to achieve what this person has achieved?

- What return on investment (ROI) can you expect from working with this coach?

- Are the answers you need already available from experienced leaders in my company?

- What is it that you want, specifically? What support do you feel you need from a coach?

- How are you going to implement the new skills you learn?

These questions are important, because so many newbies spend all their money on coaches rather than doing the activities necessary to make money and find success. Look closely at where you are in the business *right now*. If I'm diving into social media, I'm going to pick a coach who's already super successful in that area. If you're just starting out, don't choose a coach who spends most of their time talking about scaling five-figure monthly residual income to six. Come back to that coach in six months or whenever you get to that stage in your business. What do you need *right now*? Find someone who can help you get it. Do your research. *Do I like what this person does? Do I share their message?* If not, keep looking.

I wouldn't be here without the coaches who pushed me to invest in myself and my family. The right coach can be the catalyst to action. A kick in the rear. A hand to hold. Someone to show you the ropes so you don't waste money or time. But the wrong one can leave you with a business owner's nightmare—more money going out than coming in. Choose wisely, sister.

CHAPTER 3

HOW TO BUILD (OR REBUILD) YOUR BUSINESS

In my eight years in business, the number one question I always get asked is, *Kacie, what exactly are you doing?* I'm not talking high-level overview. These women want the nitty-gritty, the real and raw, the step by step, the tried-and-true way to build a network marketing business. They're asking me to be their boss. To the women I believe will stick it out, I say, "I can tell you what to do . . . if and only if you're ready."

So let me lead you and show you exactly what I did. Don't freak out. I know, I know. You didn't start your own business to have a boss. Nor do you ever want to clock in with me. I won't ask you to. Just know that a healthy direction is *always* good. After working with thousands of women over the past ten years and surrounding myself with high-caliber leaders, I understand that we need direction, coaching, and support in our businesses.

Do you want to figure this out on your own? Enough said. So let's go back to my first days in this industry so you can see what it takes to build a business that lasts.

WHY YOUR ORIGIN STORY IS YOUR NUMBER ONE ASSET

Bear with me. I know what the critics will say.

"But Kacie, I don't sell essential oils."

"I don't care about the product as much as the community aspect."

"What does my story have to do with anything?"

The heart of your business is the product. If you do not 110 percent believe in what you are selling, you will fail. As you read my story, I want you to consider yours. What's your conviction? How has your product changed your life? Dig deep and get clear. This skill will be your number one asset.

When I was eighteen years old, I moved from Wyoming to Denver to go to college. Right next to my house was a cute little hippy shop. They sold tie-dyes, incense, clothing, jewelry, and other "interesting" things. In the back corner by the Bob Marley posters sat this little essential oil stand. My first time in the shop, I uncapped and smelled all forty oils. I left with a few and enough loose change to buy a week's worth of ramen noodles, white bread, and eggs. Patchouli, frankincense, and sandalwood made the low-quality meals worth it.

With next month's allowance from my parents, I bought the book displayed next to the oils—*Introduction to Aromatherapy*.

Growing up, I struggled with anxious and sad feelings. I had my first panic attack in first grade. Back then they didn't discuss emotional issues. You felt what you felt; it was what it was. So I told no one. I didn't know anything was wrong with me.

That changed when I read the book. It turns out patchouli, frankincense, and sandalwood were the right oils for me. I had no idea at the time. I bought them to use as perfume because I liked their smell. The days I massaged the oils into my skin, my anxious feelings faded. The days I forgot, it came pounding back.

I put a few drops of patchouli in the shower one day, breathed in the calming steam, and looked in the mirror. *I haven't felt this good in a really long time. It's got to be these oils.*

Every month I added a new oil to my collection until I was well stocked and confident in the product for every use. When I got my bachelor's degree and moved to Bozeman, Montana, for graduate school, I had to find a replacement oil shop. Lucky for me, an essential oil shop was a short walk from my new campus. As in Denver, I was there with every spare dollar I had buying oils. I still have the little budget sheet I made with all the oil names and prices with check marks next to the ones I'd bought.

I quickly became friends with the owner. One day she shared with me that she was putting the shop up for sale. My heart raced. *Forget grad school. I'm going to buy this essential oil shop in downtown Bozeman. I'll be a business owner before I'm twenty-five.*

I walked into the shop a week later, and the owner greeted me like any other day.

"Hey, I'm interested in purchasing your shop," I said.

"Interested? In buying all this?" The owner looked down at me over her blue-framed bifocals. "Really?"

"Yeah, really. Maybe we can sit down and run the numbers. I don't know about any business loans, but I know I can get the money together from my family so—"

"I doubt you could get a loan from any bank. I'm just looking to sell my inventory, really."

"Oh, gosh . . . wow . . . I love your store."

"Thank you, Kacie. That means a lot to me."

"I just—" I looked down at the oil display next to the cash register. "I've absolutely fallen in love with these oils. Maybe I can still save the store."

"I wish you could. But you'd probably go bankrupt before you sign the papers." She wiped her glasses with the corner of her cardigan. "Aren't you a student? I'm sure you have a promising career ahead of you. Don't give it all up on a whim."

I didn't buy the shop. The owner closed her doors a few months before I finished grad school. Soon after graduation, I landed a job teaching at the university. In the meantime, I'd gotten married and had two kids—Emma and Sulli. Around Sulli's second birthday, he came down with an ear infection.

Our family doctor diagnosed Sulli with recurrent otitis media (chronic ear infection) and put him on amoxicillin. After ten days he was better. Then it came back. This cycle continued on for two months. On round three, Sulli had an allergic reaction—a common side effect. His little body broke out in welts that looked like second-degree burns. Then the welts turned black, and his face swelled to the size of a basketball. I was devastated.

I called the doctor and got the first appointment I could. When we got there, the nurse shrugged off my worry—and my tears.

"The doctor isn't concerned. This is just an allergic reaction we commonly see. We're going to give you a steroid cream to apply to your son's skin. Keep in mind that this will make his skin very sensitive, and it could potentially tear."

"*Tear*? Like . . ." I got choked up. "Isn't there something else we can do?"

"Yes. We recommend that you meet with an ear, nose, and throat specialist to go over options for tubes and possible adenoid removal."

I freaked. I took Sulli to an ENT doctor.

"Your son's ear canals are tilted," the ENT said. "Scar tissue has built up, so he will always struggle with ear infections. His hearing loss will, unfortunately, get worse and continue to get worse. All we can recommend is surgery to remove scar tissue and put tubes in his ears. We'll get that surgery on the schedule as soon as possible. See you back here in two weeks for his preoperative appointment."

I cried all the way out to the car. My son just stared at me wide-eyed. This wasn't working for us anymore. It was time I went back to what I knew in my heart worked. If I was going to help Sulli, I needed to find the sweet spot where Western medicine and a natural approach to health care meet.

As soon as I got home, I reached out to a girlfriend who'd just started her own essential oil business.

"What do you recommend for an ear infection?" I asked her.

"Melaleuca. Sulli needs melaleuca. It's tea tree oil. It dries stuff up naturally. And lavender for his skin."

"Tea tree oil." I was very familiar with it but never liked the smell, so I hadn't bought it. I felt defeated. "I don't have any I'm confident about using on my son."

"Don't worry. I'll overnight some to you."

Two days later, I massaged melaleuca around Sulli's ears. That night was the first since I could remember he didn't wake me up screaming. He slept through each night two weeks straight.

At the preoperative appointment, the same nurse looked into Sulli's ears. Twice. She shook her head.

"Mom to mom . . ."

Oh, boy.

"Look at that picture on the wall of a healthy ear. Now, look in your son's ear." She handed me the otoscope.

I looked in Sulli's ears, then back at the picture.

"They look exactly the same," I said.

"Yes."

"So . . . is he better?"

"The doctor will be in to speak with you shortly."

When the doctor examined Sulli's ears, he said the words every mother wants to hear.

"There is absolutely no reason to go through with the surgery. I don't know what you're doing. Quite frankly, I don't want to know because it would put me out of business. But keep doing it." He walked out of the room smiling.

Sulli hasn't had an ear infection since. He does have selective hearing, but that was there before the ear infections. I have a theory about the cause, but that's an issue for a different book.

I called my girlfriend on the drive home from the preop. "I want a bottle of this stuff every month. Sign me up." For my first year working with essential oils, I considered myself a customer, not a business builder. I committed to a monthly order. For Christmas I bought myself the biggest kit they sell, the one for people who want to turn their oil passion into a business. At the time, I had no idea that would be my future.

I loved essential oils for eighteen years before I ever sold a bottle. I studied, sampled, and experienced so many life-altering benefits that I couldn't help but share. I wasn't thinking about making money. And I wasn't considering running a business. Selling oils wasn't on my dream career list. Yet my passion for the product may well be the most important asset to my success. The same goes for you. If you *believe* in skin care, travel, or healthy weight loss, then live the lifestyle before you build the business. Your conviction, your passion, and your story are all you need.

BLOW THE DUST OFF YOUR VISION

I started with a vision board. You probably did, too. Yours is behind your desk collecting dust waiting to be found and conquered. Get that baby out. Let the vision serve you. If your vision board is designed with clear intention, it will kick you into full-blown action and make you unstoppable. Every time you look at the mountaintop, the beautiful beach home, the fancy car, the desired yoga pose, you get to work. Head down. Vision-driven. And if you are one of those whose doesn't light a fire, you need one regardless. Let me show you why.

When you're pursuing a vision, you have intention in every action you do. The business you're building. The people you're hanging with. The conversations you're having. The way you're spending your money. The person you're becoming. Everything falls into alignment with what you want your future to hold, and you make it so. Without a vision, we live in a space where we feel bored, we hate our work, and we drag through life. If that feels like you, it's time to go back to the drawing board. Well, the vision board, I should say. Examine your life. Ask, *Where do I want to be tomorrow, in thirty days, in sixty days, in ninety days . . . in a year? Where do I see myself with my spouse? Where do I see my kiddos? Where do I see our financial future? Where do I see everything?* Break your vision down into all these different pieces. Get intentional at the drawing board of your life. Refocus, revamp, redo. That's why it's so important to revisit your vision often in your life. Otherwise we forget where we're going, and we've got to start over. Visualize your business success every day. With intention comes focus. With focus comes results.

I could talk about visions all day long. But now I need to be real with you for a minute. Vision boards are important, but they're not *strategy*. Designing a vision board is *not* a money-making activity. You won't get instant results. An increase in your paycheck. Prospective buyers banging down your door. Nope. However, your vision board will guide you to create the exact plan to achieve your goals and desires. Let the vision create your plan.

What do I mean by a plan? My first week in business, I got out my calculator and sketch pad and looked over the company compensation plan. Since I knew how much I needed to break free from my current situation—$5,000 per month—all I had to do was run the numbers. *Here's the rank I need to reach. Here's the number of products I need to sell. The amount of contacts I need to make. The number of enrollments I need to have. The number of partners I need. Here's what my monthly growth has to look like.*

Around the same time, I was reading a book my girlfriend gave me—*Beach Money* by Jordan Adler, a seven-figure network marketer. This was my first multilevel marketing experience, so I had no idea what to expect. My girlfriend kept telling me I could make a ton of money and live a different lifestyle, but like all newbies, I wanted to know *how*. In the book, Jordan says that if you commit two straight years to this business, your life will never be the same. You can make fast cash a lot sooner than that. But you're not going to create the residual income and retirement fund people wish they could brag about until you commit to a strategy for a length of time.

THE FIVE TO EIGHT RULE

I took Jordan's idea to heart and broke down my plan. I'm going to talk to five to eight new people every single week. If I'm committing to two years, I will never miss a week. Maybe I introduce friends coming over to my house to the product. Maybe I go to a networking event. Maybe I teach one of those online classes and advertise. Whatever. I'll figure it out.

For two straight years, I made good on my promise. I never missed a week. Ever. All because I knew how many people I needed to talk to and in what time frame. These numbers may not be what your compensation plan requires, and that's OK. I chose these numbers based on the results I wanted. Choose what works best for you. What doesn't change depending on specific goals is what doesn't work in this industry. If you want to make it, dreaming, hoping, and praying isn't the way, friend. Every outcome you desire is tied to an activity you can do.

Those activities need to be consistent. If two years feels like too much commitment, break it down to ninety days. Every week for three months, talk to five to eight new people. Anyone can do that for ninety days. Stick with it for those ninety days and you've got yourself a new habit.

Most aspiring network marketers don't make it to the magical two-year mark. Most quit after six months. It's a shame. Six to nine months in our industry is a sweet spot. People are watching you. They're waiting to see you if you stick it out. Jump ship. Keep using the product. Make any money. You have a following, and you must show up to the party. If you don't commit to activities that guarantee residual income (or just do them sporadically), you kill your momentum. I talked to five people last week, and nothing happened. Might as well give this up. Not every person you talk to will buy from you. Anyone could tell you that. Remind yourself, I'm going to do this every week for two consecutive years. If you don't, you'll get discouraged, quit, and show up in another MLM. I've seen people go from makeup to cleaning products back to makeup in the space of a year. Why not pick one company with a product you love and stick to a strategy that works?

THE POWER OF STRUCTURE: A DAY IN THE LIFE OF A SUCCESSFUL NETWORK MARKETER

One of the first hard lessons I learned in this industry is that professional goals with hobby hours doesn't cut it. You should probably underline that statement. Success is scheduled, friend. This makes my story different. With most MLM compensation plans, ten to fifteen hours a week is realistic to make $5,000 a month. If anyone tells you that they earn that (or more) working less, I guarantee that's not the only thing they're lying to you about. The good news is, you can find these ten to fifteen hours in your current lifestyle. That's what I did in the beginning. I made time for phone calls while I was driving, and I met people between classes on campus.

So, what does my typical day look like? That depends. On me. On my kids. On my family. And on my calendar. I have the choice every single day. Most mornings, I get up between six and seven. I make coffee, enjoy a few minutes to myself before the kiddos jump out of bed, and glance at my calendar to get an idea of what my day looks like. At eight thirty, I go for a hike with my dogs, lift weights in our gym, or attend a barre class. By ten, I've showered and I'm ready to begin my workday. I don't schedule any phone calls before ten. My mornings are for me and for my family.

From 10:00 a.m. until 3:00 p.m. when I pick up our youngest son, Sulli, I hit this business *hard*. I have a planner that outlines exactly what's going on in my day, whether that's holding team calls, showing up for strategy sessions, following up, sharing the business, or connecting with my business manager. It's all in my planner. No guesswork. At three, I pick up Emma and Sulli, and we chat about our days until four. Then while they do homework, I work for another hour.

On Mondays and Fridays, I spend most of my work time doing office stuff. I catch up on emails and mail product samples to customers who have requested them. I also create content such as newsletters, social media posts, and video trainings. On Tuesdays, Wednesdays, and Thursdays, I'm head down into money-making activities, which include sharing the product, following up with prospects, teaching classes, enrolling new customers, and mentoring my team.

Just about every evening, I spend time with my family. We'll play in the garden, cook dinner together, walk the dogs, go on a bike ride, sit on the deck, or enjoy the hot tub. There are a couple of minor exceptions. Monday nights I have a thirty-minute team call. Tuesday evenings I teach classes, schedule sales calls, or run live webinars. This set schedule prepares my family for what's to come. Clear expectations mean no surprises.

By the end of the week, I've accomplished what needs to happen in a thirty- to forty-hour workweek. Don't get me wrong—not everyone in this industry chooses to work that much, nor do they have to. That's the beauty of it. My hours are in complete alignment with my goals. For you, it may be two to five hours a week for an extra couple hundred dollars. Make sure that when you set up your schedule, you're clear on what the result looks like. You're not going to make $100,000 a month working ten hours a week.

I'll be honest. Sometimes I need a break. That's why I love this business. Some days I do nothing to grow my business, and that's OK. It's a perk of creating momentum and building a business with residual income. *You* get to choose when you work and when you don't.

Does my job stop while I'm spending evenings and weekends with my family? Absolutely not. I'm always sharing my products. And when women find out how much my business earns, they always say, "How are you doing that? Please tell me everything!"

The first thing I always tell people is to align your expectations with a system. Second, make sure you pick a product you care about. If you're selling activewear but spend most of your free time on the sofa, your message won't resonate with anyone. Join the right business and follow the right system to build it and you *cannot* fail. It's just not possible. That doesn't mean life is a grind. When you're marketing right, selling right, and recruiting right, everything is a lot easier.

On top of ten to fifteen hours working on your business, commit one hour a week to product education. Keep tabs on your company. What new products can you sell? What new uses can you tell customers about? What new studies or statistics support your product? And why does any of this matter to your target market? Focus on one lesson every week and blow it up—share what you learn with everyone you know who could use your product, whether it's an essential oil, acne cream, or a supplement. Remember, stories sell. Share your testimonials and before and after of using the product. Those are the conversations that stick with people.

Think about the last time someone posted a before and after example on social media of a teenager's acne, a child's scraped knee, or a success story around weight loss. It inspired you to want to reach out and ask questions. Individualized care like this makes network marketing amazing. It doesn't matter what you're selling. People will seek your advice and expertise to lead them in the right direction. Know your stuff. When I'm on top of the latest research, I can't help but tell every person in my life about the products and how they can impact their life. Knowledge is contagious. And the conviction you convey when you're confident makes other people want to create their own story.

Don't get me wrong—it's easy to get off the path of staying in the know. As you grow, it's easy to lose sight of your passion. You can become overwhelmed quickly. You're motivating your builders, staying organized, meeting new people, and trying to have a personal life. To remind yourself why you're doing MLM in the first place, go back to school. By this I mean do your homework. Study the different ways your product can help people, engage with multiple experts in your company, and watch what other top leaders do. Share that information with as many people as you can. The next person you talk to, ask what's going on in their world. What are they struggling with? Take that problem, research it, mail a sample, and follow up to see how it worked. Do that with everyone you meet and you'll never have to ask what to research next. Best of all, you'll have fun.

I've realized that if you're not in the flow of using and loving your product, you're not out talking about it. If you're not passionate about using what you're selling, you're not selling it.

All that said, a schedule is just as important as product passion and knowledge. Why? Because without a schedule, you can't stick with anything for ninety days, much less two years. Remember your last New Year's resolution about doing Pilates twice a week? Maybe you stuck with it for a month. How long did it take until you were down to working out once a week, then skipping it altogether? *I have all these dishes in the sink; I'd better stay home. I have to pick up the kids from soccer practice; I'll just fit an extra session in next week.* If you don't make an activity part of your schedule, it doesn't happen. What about your kiddo's checkups or your hair color appointment? You never skip those. That's because you committed to them when—you guessed it—you put them on your schedule. Do the same with your business and you won't be tempted to skip them. If you need inspiration for your schedule, look at mine.

Weekly Planner   Week: Sample Week Approx. 20 Hours

Monday	Tuesday	Wednesday	Thursday	Friday	Saturday	Sunday
Personal Development 15mins	Personal Development 15mins	Personal Development 15mins	Personal Development 15mins	Personal Development 15mins	Personal Development 15mins	Personal Development 15mins
3 Hours of Office Time	1-2 Hours Product or Business Education	1 Hour Meet with people	2 Hours Srategy Session with Key Builders	3 Hours of Office Time		
	1 hr Contact / Follow Up / Share	1 Hour Customer Appreciation - Continuing Education			1 hr Contact / Follow Up / Share	
			1 hr Contact / Follow Up / Share			
1 hr Contact / Follow Up / Share						
Social Media Content 15mins	Social Media Content 15mins	Social Media Content 15mins	Social Media Content 15mins	Social Media Content 15mins	Social Media Content 15mins	Social Media Content 15mins
Team Call		Class or Event				

Success is scheduled. With success comes a lot of responsibilities. I don't function well when I'm all over the place. Do you? It's crucial that you keep your headspace clear and designate the important tasks. Since my goals shift often, my focus must shift as well. Where do I want to go with this business now? Where do I want to go with my personal life? I've dialed down my daily tasks so I can stay organized and clear the cobwebs. That's how I stay true to my goal and stay on track to achieve it.

If I lose clarity, I set aside time to refocus on my priorities and what it takes to make them happen. I'm grateful I'm in an industry where I can spend three or four weeks working through this and still (a) have a job and (b) get to spend time with my family. Once my head is clear, I'm ready to roll. That probably goes for you, too—time away makes you more productive.

Remember, this is normal. Schedule quarterly reviews so you can analyze your goals, what you've achieved, what's not working, where you want to go, and (if it makes sense) how you need to re-create your vision. When you don't revisit your business plan regularly, you become stagnant, and your growth stops. A successful business evolves. You must evolve with it.

(NEARLY) UNBREAKABLE BOUNDARIES

When you're running a business at home, it's tempting to let household activities distract you. But when the clothes dryer buzzer goes off, and you stop whatever you're doing to change the laundry, you'll lose your momentum. Would an employer let you do that? I don't think so. Don't multitask. Research shows that multitasking makes every task take 40 percent longer.[1]

That's because you're not multitasking, you're switching back and forth between tasks. The laundry can wait until your lunch break. It's your responsibility to be your own boss now.

On that same note, it's important that family and friends honor your set hours. Separate personal time from business. If somebody wants to get together and talk about their spouse or their kiddos, I don't want that conversation on my calendar during work hours. Once again, would an employer put up with that? If you want to talk friendship, let's do it right and have fun—when business hours are over. I'll chat about anything you want. If this sounds heartless, well, it isn't. I want all of my best friends doing business with me. But if all we did was chitchat and not make money, none of us would survive. Remember, we're creating a duplicative model. How we run our business is how our builders will run theirs.

Do the rules change if you have kids? Most women on my team are moms. It's all well and good to ignore the dryer buzzer, but what about mom guilt? The best way to keep your family happy and healthy while still blowing up your income is, once again, a consistent schedule. The structure of a schedule creates predictability, which inspires respect from kiddos and spouses alike. Kids appreciate the fact that their parents are functioning individuals in society. When they see us succeed, they want to succeed, too. They won't be mad because they know you're not skipping a meeting so you can color with them. My only exception is for emergencies. I show up for my kids when they need me. I have no problem saying, "I'm sorry, my son's taken a tumble, and I need to end our call. Can I follow up with you soon?" People get it.

Eight to nine months into your commitment to this consistency, you'll feel like a business owner. You'll get hooked on the momentum you've been building, and you'll want more. Yes, it takes that long to create residual income. It's the hard truth, sister, and that's the only kind there is. Women who quit MLM before that eight- to nine-month mark never built the structure necessary to see the results that are possible. They have no plan, no set number of hours a week, and no idea how many people to talk to. They get stuck in micromanagement. They find time for everything except money-making activities. Vision boards, affirmations, motivational seminars, you name it. Network marketing is like any other job. If an activity isn't making you money, you shouldn't waste time on it. Even today, I catch women hounding people on social media. *Who's sick today? I'm going to spend fourteen hours on Facebook finding that one sick person. Then I'll pitch my product.* If social media increases your paycheck, amazing. But if you're just going to message someone with a headache, acne, or a sore back, you will not put food on your table. Don't waste your time wasting theirs.

Your schedule is only as impactful as the activities you fit into it. If you're going to let me coach you, you deserve to know what I expect. Same as what I expected of myself. The money-making activities that got me to $5,000 in residual income per month got my business to seven figures in sales every year. I simply increased my hours per week from ten to fifteen up to forty. I didn't become a workaholic. I don't neglect my family. I set boundaries around my work hours, and I do my best to stay consistent and true to my business obligations. And every week,

I talk to five to eight new people. No matter what. So what, exactly, are those money-making activities?

THE ESSENTIAL MONEY-MAKING ACTIVITIES

You already know that every single week, you're going to talk to five to eight new people. But your connection with them doesn't end there.

FOLLOWING THE FIVE TO EIGHT RULE

The next week, you'll follow up with the ones you talked to the previous week by sending them samples or reaching out to find out how the sample worked for them. So every week you're talking to new people and following up with the ones you met the week before. You're keeping the cycle going by always working on the previous week's people and connecting to this week's new people. And at the end of the month, you'll have at least eight to ten new customers. Run this system every week for two years and you're on track to own a multimillion-dollar business.

If direct sales success is this simple, why don't more women make it? Because the Five to Eight Rule goes against what everybody else is doing. They're playing the numbers game, and most of them are losing. The Five to Eight Rule sets you apart from other women in this industry because it's about *quality*, not *quantity*. Yes, you want those five to eight connections, but if they're people who have no interest in what you're selling, they're poor-quality leads. If you talk to a hundred people one week but none of them would buy from you, it's pointless. You're much better off spending the time on people who *want* to hear about what you're selling.

Personally, I love building my business through one-on-ones or small group settings. I'm an introvert, so that's my preference. For me, making small talk is unbelievably challenging. My husband is a total extrovert. He could talk to anybody, sell anything, and go home happy and content. Not me. I prefer small groups. If I could get invited over to a friend's house to drink a glass of wine and talk books, kids, or life, odds are I'll meet new people. Boom. I get my five to eight in one setting. Otherwise, I may schedule a few one-on-one coffee or lunch dates throughout the week with women I haven't seen in a long time or with people I meet on social media, at the grocery store, or at my daughter's school. Whatever it takes to have a conversation with five to eight people, I'm game.

Most people find their five to eight people organically when they get out of the house, meaning you probably don't have to plan them into your schedule. Anybody can do this, even if you don't know that many people. Expand your circle of influence, sister. Not just for business but for your own personal well-being. Get out and do things you love. If you enjoy reading, go to the library or join a book club. If you want to surround yourself with like-minded go-getters, join a networking group. It was at the business networking group I joined early on where I learned how to dial down my long-winded oils description into a "thirty-second commercial." During my half-minute pitch, I would talk about a pain spot everyone could relate to (headaches), what I would suggest (peppermint essential oil), and how to learn more (talk to me after the meeting). Amazing things happen when you tell people how you can help them. What does your product do? Don't be shy about its uses and benefits. Soon your five to eight people will *come to you.*

LISTENING FOR THE TOP THREE COMPLAINTS

So you're ready to talk to five to eight new people every week. Great. Now, what do you say? Well . . . not much. Not at first. You *listen.* The number one skill in business is listening. When you hear what people want—and trust me, they'll tell you—you can meet their needs. For example, if your product helps with aging, you're watching your friends suffer through the process, and you don't offer to help, that's freaking selfish. If you have something that works, it's your duty to share it. How can you *not* share your product with five to eight people a week? You have an obligation to listen and share.

Whether you're at the grocery store, the gym, or your office, you hear women complain about the same three things. Women want to talk about their finances, their physical health, and their emotional well-being. "I'm broke, sick, and sad." If you have a product that helps relieve any of these pains, *help them.* That's the beauty of the Five to Eight Rule. This is an organic business, remember? You have a whole week. You're not setting a timer and telling yourself, *OK, I have to push my products on two people in the next forty-five minutes.* Everywhere you go, you're listening, and you're sharing. If you're taking your kiddos on a play date, going to yoga, or going out for wine with your girlfriends, take that opportunity to listen. It's the heart-centered, feminine approach to building a business. If you take a moment to listen to the people around you, opportunities flood into your life like campaign ads during election week.

When you listen to someone, you know what they want. If the woman in front of you in line at the DMV spends fifteen minutes telling you about her divorce, then you know she needs something to help lift her mood. Don't push a sale—she'll think you're trying to benefit from her misery. Say, "Can we exchange phone numbers? There's something I'd really like to share with you that I have at home." If you have the sample with you, even better. Then you can say, "Can I call you in a few days? I'd love to know if it helps you feel better."

Everywhere I go, I listen with compassion, and I speak with passion. I don't cold-call (not that it's wrong), hit up old friends from high school, or peruse social media to pitch that one person who is sick today. I stay true to who I am. I maintain my integrity and show up in this space and this life. I live the lifestyle I believe in.

SHARING YOUR PRODUCT WITH LOVE

Whenever you hear someone complain about a problem you can solve—aging, menstrual cramps, low libido, adult acne, whatever—get them sampling your products right away. In my business, we give newcomers an experience with our products. If I'm at a salon, and the woman next to me talks about her migraine, I'll share my product with her on the spot. Then she gets an immediate experience. If I'm catching up with a friend on the phone, and she says, "I'm really struggling with my bowels these days," I mail her a sample (on a Monday or Friday, of course).

If people don't have an experience with the product or see a true testimonial, they're probably not going to buy it. It's best to provide an immediate experience so you can capitalize on their interest and need as soon as possible. I don't mean hand them a sign-up sheet. That's salesy. What you will do is take care of them. Love on them. Ease the discomfort in their lives. You listen, build a relationship, and become part of their world. Once you've established trust, invite them to an event you already have scheduled.

All of your sharing should come without expectation. If you push for a sale, you'll turn people off instantly. When I share my product with someone, I intend to make a difference in that person's life. When I made that shift in my thinking, my business exploded from five figures to six, then to seven. When we act out of desperation—"Hey, I'm going to give you this sample today, call you tomorrow, and enroll you the day after"—people freak out. And with good reason. When I give out a sample, I genuinely want the person to go home and use it. I want them to fall in love with it, and I want them to have an experience.

CIRCLING BACK EVERY WEEK

Once people try your sample, a good number of them will come back to you and ask for more before you even have the chance to follow up. That's great. That's when you transition from sharing to selling. In my experience, this is the hardest shift for women to make. That's why so many of us get stuck at the six-month mark. We sink in debt from buying products we gave away. We haven't sold a thing. In the next chapter, I'm going to retrain your brain to see money and sales in a fresh new way.

For now, I want you meeting, sampling, and following up with five to eight new people a week. That's five to eight new touches plus five to eight follow-ups from the previous week. After you've given them a sample in person or as your follow-up, circle back to make sure they're using the product properly.

Customer service is *everything* in this business. It's the difference between making a million dollars and going broke in six months. Yet I see so many women share a sample or, yes, even sell a product, and they don't follow up. They literally let income *walk away*. If you don't follow up to see how they're doing, that's lame. No one wants to buy from someone like that. Think they'll ever come back and buy from you if you don't bother to ask how they feel a week after they've enjoyed your free sample?

In a world where anyone can order anything on Amazon for a fraction of the cost, how do retail stores stay in business? Excellent customer service. They offer an experience that clicking "buy now" can't beat. It's real human connection and real help for real people. That's what your future customers care about, and that's what they're willing to spend their money on.

Customer service done right builds trust and forms relationships. Maybe that woman with irritated bowels just orders here and there, but I know she's telling everyone in her family, at church, and at her doctor's office about me. Then the referrals come. It's noon on a Tuesday, and I've gotten multiple calls from her friends wanting products to support their digestive health. That's another way your business will grow. There is no such thing as "tapping out my warm market." If you're upping your customer service game, people can't help but talk about you. Then you'll have the confidence to ask for referrals without feeling slimy.

"Who else do you know that might need my help?"

If you're going to sample and sell your way to a seven-figure business, watch your retention rate. If you're providing awesome customer service, if you're providing the product education your customers deserve, if you're teaching them the lifestyle of using your product to enrich their life, then they'll be lifetime members. I don't want people buying products, putting them in their medicine cabinet or jewelry shelf, and never looking at them again. I want people falling in love with what I offer because I've helped them make a true life change. And when that happens, it's no longer just product samples changing hands; it's putting food on your table and providing for your family—and everybody can feel good about that.

CHAPTER 4

THE ULTIMATE MONEY-MAKING ACTIVITY

Sales. Women fear it. And men love it. Makes little sense. Women are masters of selling. We blow men out of the freaking water. Not my opinion. A review of thirty thousand sales calls found that women close 11 percent more deals than men.[1] Not surprising. Women sell every day. We sell ourselves on getting up early to make coffee, for example. *If I get up at five-thirty and put a fresh pot on, I'll have enough time to shave my legs.* Two hours later, we sell our kids on breakfast. "Emma, I know you don't like tuna, but guess what? Today you're eating it, and here's why. You're going to get all these omegas that will make doing your homework easier. And if you eat it all, you can take a muffin in your lunch." Two pitches, two sales, and it's not even 8:00 a.m.

Women can sell anything anywhere to anyone while accomplishing any task. Men can't do that. My husband can't do two things at once. I, however, take my kids to the playground, meet new friends, share a sample, schedule an appointment, and sell some products. Every woman has this in her. Yet there's a disconnect. Giving out free products is easy. Asking for money is hard. That's a problem, and I'm going to show you how to overcome it.

At a national MLM conference I attended, a couple ran a breakout workshop on selling. They got up on stage and pulled out every way to talk about selling without mentioning money.

"Friends, just think of yourself as *serving*."

This statement got me thinking. What does that even mean? Why must we not see sales for what it is? And how do we take this concept and apply it to our business without carrying guilt about our desires or goals? With everyone on social media echoing similar sentiments about sales, it's no wonder it's hard for us to say things like, "I would love to make a million dollars a year." But you know what's *easy* for women to say? "I don't need that kind of money." I'm scratching my head. Are you?

So the question goes like this: Why would you *not* want to make a million dollars a year? Or be successful so you can share more? The more money you make, the more you can help other people. Wanting more money doesn't mean putting it all in your pocket for lattes and manicures. What about your favorite charity? What about the little box at the grocery store that collects donations for the local animal shelter? What about that letter from your kid's school asking for help to repair the gym? Fear stops many women from answering.

When you're not selling what you should, fear gets loud. Sell products, and fear doesn't mean a thing. So why tiptoe around sales? Let's cut the fear (and guilt) about selling our products. Hold yourself to a higher standard. To me, serving is a *giving* behavior. And sales is the most effective and efficient way to empower someone to own the product and live the lifestyle you are sharing. Not giving away freebies. *Selling.* Sharing samples has an important place in the sales process, but too many women end transactions with, "Try this and let me know what you think." If you don't follow up, what happens next? Your friend takes that lavender, loves it, wants more, and stands in her local natural food market feeling overwhelmed by all the choices. So she buys the cheapest version, gets no results, and ends up as a nonbeliever.

You wouldn't believe how often this happens. You *know* the product works. Heck, your friend knows the products work, too. But the second you have to ask for money, you get all freakish, and your palms get sweaty. Sound familiar? Don't worry, sister. You are *not* alone.

When someone tells you they love your sample, all you have to say is, "Of course you do. I knew you would. Let me show you the easiest and most cost-effective way to get more." It's important to tell people what service they're getting when they buy from you. That's the beauty of network marketing— you cut the middleman out. People want the education. They want to know why they should buy this versus that. If they buy something at Target, they don't get any product education, they don't get the customer service, and they definitely don't get the relationship. That's why direct selling is the most empowering thing a woman can do for other women.

Still, women struggle with exchanging money. We don't want people thinking we're selfish. *I'm sorry I have to make a living. I'm sorry I have to ask you to pay for what I'm selling you.* Please. Men are a different story. My husband goes out and makes a million-dollar deal and doesn't even question it. He's salivating over that bonus. To get a woman to sell something, she needs to know she's going to make an impact. Every single dollar that enters my bank account represents the impact I've made. The same goes for your network marketing business. When you sell a product to someone, you're not just impacting that one individual. You're impacting their entire circle of influence. That person takes your product—an essential oil, skin care, a supplement—and tells fifteen friends. Those people contact you so they can try it, too. Then the cycle starts again. They love it, so they turn around and tell fifteen more people about it. You're having such a positive impact on other people's lives. *You deserve compensation.* That's how we need to see money. Money represents value. If we don't associate selling with creating value, we're doing ourselves a disservice.

Think about it—when we know something works, when we know we can change someone's life with a product, it's our obligation to sell that product. I used oils to relieve my anxiety, get over depression, and help my son while everyone else around me was sick and miserable. A girlfriend told me I was selfish for not sharing. She was right.

BECOMING THE PRODUCT OF THE PRODUCT

When you become a product of the product, you don't need to worry about getting "pushy." People know the benefits you're getting. And they know exactly what you're selling. Network marketing isn't just about a single product. It's about wellness, support, community, purpose, and impact. People are watching it all, which is why it's so important to always walk the walk.

When you're the product of the product, you become the go-to person in your circle of influence. You're living the lifestyle your neighbors want to live. It won't take long for them to reach out to you and ask for advice. Take personal trainers. They're great examples of being a product of the product. They practice what they preach. Do you think they're at the gym regularly? Of course. People reach out to them for advice because they live the lifestyle they sell—the life other people want.

When you have a quality product, one you believe in and use often, you're more than a salesperson. You're a *messenger*. When you have an important message, you can talk all day long. Think about it—when you have a good thing, you share it. That's being a messenger. This is what we do as women. Selling is our natural behavior. The only difference is now you're going to accept money for what you sell. And yes, you're going to start selling.

THE SALES SKILLS YOU ALREADY HAVE

Isn't it funny how we miss what's obvious to everyone else?

"I don't have the skills to start a business on the side," my girlfriend told me. "I mean, it would be amazing to spend more time with women. And I'd love to get out more socially. My friends are always complaining I'm becoming antisocial. And I do love the product. But I have no idea how to make money. I'm definitely *not* a salesperson. I mean, I wish I could leave my job so I'd have more time to do what I love. I'm just not ready."

"Uh, scheduling your time? That's crucial for business. You have more than enough skills," I said. "You also take care of your family and your home, and you do a good job. You deserve to take care of yourself, too."

"I don't know." She looked down at her hands. "I can't imagine up and quitting my job right now. What do I know about business?"

"Way more than you realize. Running a business isn't that different from running a household. You're basically the project manager of your home. And you manage to keep your boss satisfied because you work so hard. If you ask me, you have more than the necessary skills to do this business with me."

She thought for a moment. "What would it look like for me to get started?"

How many times do we have this exact conversation? A ton, right? Do you give your girlfriend a hug and wish her luck? Heck no. You take this opportunity to demonstrate why she is a perfect fit for this industry. Here's the thing. Sales can be intimidating. Start with honoring that and then have an honest conversation on why this industry can be a fit for every single individual if they align what they already know with what is necessary to find success.

So what are some of the skills necessary to be successful in sales?

- Passion for the product—sell what you love
- Desire to build relationships—this is a relationship business
- Positive—this industry is a blast, and that should be your number one focus
- Coachable—trust the process your company and successful leaders teach you
- Time management—women are masters at this
- Goal oriented—thirty-, sixty-, and ninety-day goals and one-, two-, and five-year goals need to be clear
- Vision—what will your legacy in this company look like

SALES AND SETTING EXPECTATIONS

Just as we underestimate what we *can* do (listen and sell), we also overestimate what we *should* do (get rich quick). Same girlfriend, different conversation:

"I took to heart what you said about starting my business. I've decided to sign up with your business. I watched some of those videos online and wow . . . those women have it all. I want to make fifty thousand dollars a month, too. I think I can find five hours on the weekends to work on my business. Even though I'm employed full-time and have kiddos, basically a second job. Five hours should be enough, right? That's what people are saying."

"I'm really glad you're doing this," I said. "But fifty thousand dollars a month is an awfully big goal to start out with, especially for someone in your situation. There's no way you'll reach that working five hours a week. You could probably get there working forty hours a week."

"But that's not what this video I watched said. This lady was on a yacht with a daiquiri . . ." She trailed off. "I got duped, didn't I? I *knew* this was a bad idea."

"Hold on a minute, I didn't say that. Let's just take a step back and be real. You're a mom and have a job. To get to fifty thousand a month residual income, is your family willing to find forty hours a week for you to work? Is your employer?"

"Whoa . . ." My friend lost her breath like I'd punched her chest. "I just . . . I was definitely not expecting that much commitment. I thought I could just go out and recruit one good business builder and make a million bucks in a few years."

"That's the misconception around multilevel marketing," I said. "But it's not the reality for most people in this business. I started at fifteen hours a week and moved up to forty once I left the university. I brought in about two hundred and fifty customers and fifty builders before I got anywhere close to the big money you're talking about. It's taken me eight years to reach the top 1 percent of multilevel marketers. Most MLM entrepreneurs never get here because their expectations are all wrong. I'm not telling you not to do this; we just need to shift your expectations. Set aside some time in the beginning to learn more about the business and the products."

"Well, that's a lot more hours than what I was reading about but . . . yeah. Yeah, I think I can start at a few hundred bucks as my goal and work my way up."

"Great. And can you work ten hours a week? Maybe five hours on Saturday, five hours throughout the week?"

"I'll talk to my husband. There was a Saturday morning karate class he was thinking about taking the kids to . . . so I think we could make it work."

"Great. And who knows? Maybe one hundred dollars will turn into five hundred. Then five thousand. It just won't happen in your first month. Success is all about setting your expectations in alignment with what you're capable of doing."

Here's the thing. Success isn't easy. Anyone who ever leads you to believe it is left out crucial information about the process. Network marketing can provide time and financial freedom for you and your family as long as you set your expectations, goals, and schedule around exactly what you and your family desires. Here are the do's of clear expectations:

- Make sure *your* goal is the goal you're aligned with and not someone else's.

- Choose working hours that are manageable and attainable.

- Create financial goals within the reality of what the compensation plan and your schedule allows.

- Work with your upline or other successful industry leaders to ensure your schedule and goals are in complete alignment.

HONOR THE AWKWARD

Let's honor the awkwardness around selling. To tell you the truth, I don't think the *ick* feeling around sales ever completely goes away. Anytime we ask for money, we're going to feel it. Will you let that stop you? Do you have conviction about what you sell? Do you believe your products can help people? If you have both the conviction and the knowledge you can help people, why wouldn't you believe it? You're providing a product you *know* is life changing. In return, you're not only receiving money, you'll feel fulfilled. My heart was never this full before I started in network marketing. You should be able to say the same about this industry. If you can, you're unstoppable. You're in the right place at the right time doing the right thing. Amazing.

Once you've sold yourself on this business, you feel joy when you ask for money. Yes, *joy*. It's a rush. Today I love selling. I know what this industry provides for me and my family. In my former life, I never in a million years dreamed I'd run a successful business. If I made $5,000 a month, I could escape my marriage, get the health care my body needed, and enjoy time with my kids. That was my vision. I saw it through, and my business blew up before my eyes. Yours can, too. If you remember your why. Your vision board. The reason you're doing what you're doing. Lose sight of your vision and you may find yourself feeling awkward—and losing confidence in your product. That's why keeping your purpose front and center isn't optional, it's essential.

YOUR THREE TYPES OF CUSTOMERS (AND HOW TO SELL TO THEM)

Remember what the most important life skill is? That's right: listening. As you listen to five to eight new people every week, you not only hear what they want, you can identify the type of customer they are. Some want to buy a few products here and there; others want to build an empire alongside you. How you sell to one differs from how you sell to another. You'll still follow all the basics of listening, providing samples, and following up, but when it's time to ask for the sale, it's important to know what to expect. Distinguishing the type of person you're talking to can save you a lot of time and energy now and down the road.

That doesn't mean the one-time buyer isn't valuable. All customers are valuable. You never know how the impactful experience you provide may affect your business in the long run. Give people your utmost customer service so that when something comes up that you have a solution for, you're the first person they think of.

With that in mind, let's dive into the three customer types you'll meet out there.

THE HOBBYIST

The hobbyist is a customer, plain and simple. You'll recognize hobbyists by their initial skepticism. They won't buy from you if they haven't tried a sample first. Once they see the product work for themselves, the hobbyist loves it. If your company offers a monthly subscription, encourage the hobbyist to sign up. Make sure they know about the free training around your product's many uses so they have multiple reasons to stay a customer. Treat hobbyists right and they should account for around 75 percent of your sales.

THE SHARER

The sharer is the most valuable person we come across in the industry. You'll know them by their outgoing nature, optimistic spirit, and influential presence. When they like a product, they don't just tell family; they go live on social media and tell thousands. They'll refer people to you like crazy. They'll often provide a testimonial that speaks to the power of the product. They're not exchanging their story for money. They simply love the product and want everyone they know to love it, too. Sharers don't have the time or energy to build a business like yours, and that's OK. They'll send you people who do.

THE BUILDER

The builder samples your product and falls in love. Like the sharer, the builder has a rich circle of people they influence, but they're more aspirational. Where they are is not where they want to be. They want to supplement, replace, or blow up their current income. Builders love your product, but they *crave* your lifestyle. They see what you've been able to achieve. Now they want *in.*

Also known as leaders, qualifiers, partners, or front liners, builders are your CEOs-in-the-making. They're willing to work anywhere from five to forty hours per week, depending on the situation. Regardless of their time commitment, builders commit to consistent money-making activity. They're teachable. Committed. Driven. As you know, when you meet and enroll builders in your business, you create valuable residual income for yourself. That's why so many women chase builders (and only builders) like squirrels up a tree. Thanks a lot. Multilevel marketing earned its icky stigma because too many women pounce on hobbyists and sharers like they're builders. "This is the most amazing business opportunity for you!" Gosh, all they wanted was something for their diarrhea. They weren't asking to put in twenty hours a week working with you building a business. Not yet. They need to become products of the product first. Then they'll show up and sell products alongside you.

Most people don't want to "build a business" in today's day and age. Not even builders. They're too busy with family, kids, their current job, you name it, to think about entrepreneurship. If you meet a builder who, like you, wants to solve a pain in the world, who wants to partner with you to fulfill their vision, by all means sign them up. Just understand that the transition from customer to builder happens when they fall in love with the product. My builders never came to me asking about building a business, but that's exactly what we end up doing together.

How do we turn customers into business partners? That's the inevitable magic question that we're all dying to know the answer to. And the answer is this: the same way we get customers—by listening. I know. You were expecting some new and exciting tip to rock your world. The secret sauce to change your business forever. Nope, friend. You already know the answer. It's instinctual. It's what we do by showing up, being present, and answering a need. Listening. I promise, this skill will serve you well.

So let's break this down a bit. How many times do you hear women complaining about their financial woes? All the time, right? I mean, who couldn't use some extra money? Who doesn't feel like they're working too hard for the paycheck they're receiving? One thing has become clear to me over the last eight years. The sweet spot most women want is an extra $500 to $700 per month. Are you confident that your business structure and your leadership can help them achieve that goal? Of course you are. They already love the product. They want more money. And you have a solution.

In my entire career, fewer than twenty people have come to me and said, "I want to make thirty to fifty thousand dollars a month." They're a rarity—and a different conversation. When they do show up, it's OK to get a little nervous. Sometimes I'm stopped dead in my tracks. Here's the reality. Nothing changes besides time commitment. We work the business the same way regardless of the amount of money desired. Visions are created, plans are mapped out, schedules are dialed in, products are learned, contacts are made, follow-ups are completed, and customers, sharers, and builders are enrolled. We go from a fifteen-hour workweek to forty. It's that simple. You already know what to do.

WHAT MAKES BUILDERS DIFFERENT

You'll find that some builders aren't in it for the money. They seek community or purpose. When working with them, you keep your process the same as with other customers. Only you shift the conversation to center on their mission or purpose.

"Oh, I just want to hang out with more women," a new mom said to me at the library. "Ever since I had my daughter, I just feel so isolated. We can't really afford a sitter right now, so I mostly stay in."

Women like her—like me, like you—seek the community and collaboration that network marketing provides. It's the best part of this business—working with like-minded individuals who also aspire to achieve bigger and better things. Forming lifetime friendships. Finding true success while building toward something amazing together and leaving an impact on the world. There's nothing else like it.

Once you've established your business with hobbyists and sharers, look for builders. I mean inside your business, not outside. A common mistake in this industry is pressuring yourself to find the perfect builder rather than developing existing customers into business partners. Once we have a well-established team full of customers and sharers, builders arise, our warm market grows, and we receive a plethora of referrals. It happens every time. People fall in love with the product. People share. People want to buy the product. People sell the products. And there you have it. End of story. You've officially found partners. Ask them to join you in the business so you can show them the way.

For me, I'm looking for partners who want to stick this out for the long haul. That means I need to show up for them 110 percent and give them the guidance and support they deserve while building their business. This means I'm not going to enroll more builders than I'm capable of handling. I like to bring one to two true builders into the business a month. If you're following the Five to Eight Rule, that will happen naturally. One thing to keep in mind here is quality over quantity. When you recruit high-quality people you can invest time into, your retention rate is higher than if you'd played the numbers game. If you have a huge online presence, you risk dividing your time among hundreds of builders. Even entrepreneurially minded builders need more than a two-minute call every few weeks.

What happens often in multilevel marketing is we get so hopeful about our new customers that we lose sight of what that person wants. You know what I'm talking about. In the beginning of our business, we make a list of our top one hundred people we want to share our products with mainly by focusing on who we want to partner with. You know without a doubt that Becky will be the number one person in your organization. She's going to rock this business. She's influential. She's supercool. She's the head of the PTA. She's connected. And you finally get her to host a class. She enrolls and falls absolutely in love with the product. You invest your time, energy, and resources, prepping her for building a massive business. In your head, the stars have aligned. In Becky's, it's all about the lifestyle. You forgot one crucial component, though: to ask Becky how she sees your company fitting into her life. Becky was in it for the product, not the opportunity.

Although I'd love to spend hours and hours with all my customers, that's not the best use of my time. I plug them into every learning opportunity available, and I spend more time with those who maximize what I've already created—my builders. I don't care how big your business is. You've got to balance your time from the beginning. Empower the people you're working with so they can achieve that balance, too. Give them the tools they need to be successful, and let them rise to your level.

CHOOSING YOUR BUILDERS WITH INTENTION: EIGHT RULES FOR BUILDERS

I'm just going to say it. I don't want to partner with everyone. That's OK. Who you want on your front line may not be who I want on mine. Perfect, right? Let's put this into perspective. When you go to a job interview, the conversation and later the hiring decision are both based on personality. The boss is looking for specific traits in the individual being hired. Are you also doing the same in your business? If not, why? People often ask me how I decide who to partner and connect with. It's not always easy, but there are eight basic things I stick to.

RULE #1: YOUR BUILDERS MUST BE COOLER THAN YOU.

All the mommas reading this can attest that we don't have a lot of spare time. Who I'm spending my precious time with has to fill me up and push me to be better. If I'm spending time with someone who drains the energy out of me, I have nothing left to give myself, my kids, or my husband. So it's critical to hang out with people who step my game up, not people who tear me down.

RULE #2: YOUR BUILDERS MUST ADD VALUE.

This isn't a one-way street. Bringing value to the table is part of my job, and I love doing it. If I'm going to partner with someone, they have to bring something to the table, too. I don't know about you, but I can always use more grace, laughter, and insight. If someone is pouring a positive light into my business, I can bring my best self to every interaction. We both show up to participate. My builder attends team events, joins every call, educates themselves, and builds up their own product knowledge base. They inspire me, and vice versa. But if someone is doing nothing but taking from our relationship, showing up late or not at all, or asking the same basic questions over and over, I cut ties.

RULE #3: YOUR BUILDERS MUST BRING OUT A BETTER VERSION OF YOU.

In the beginning, I was passionate about spreading my message. I was willing to partner with anybody to expand my reach.

Although I'm still excited to share my product and impact lives, I'm now selective about who I partner with long-term. Sharing product knowledge is different from having someone on the front line. If I'm investing in someone, they need to invest in me, too. They need to challenge my assumptions, inspire me to be better, and push me to go further. When I walk away from our interaction, I'm ready to take on the world.

RULE #4: YOUR BUILDERS MUST HAVE SUPPORT AT HOME.

Think about the last time you were completely excited about something and your friends and family thought you were crazy. It made it hard to go for it and even easier to quit. If the home base isn't cheering you on, it will be challenging to justify disrupting the family routine, working at night, and traveling out of state. Network marketing requires support. If you don't get that from home, you're not likely to succeed.

RULE #5: YOUR BUILDERS MUST FEEL GOOD ABOUT MAKING MONEY.

Can we be real here for a second? If you don't like making money, don't be disappointed when you don't make any. One of the most desirable things about network marketing is you get to determine your own paycheck. With that comes creating a dream and a vision of a lifestyle you desire. You *absolutely* cannot do that if you are not willing to take payment for products you sell. Money is an exchange. Don't assign it an emotion.

RULE #6: YOUR BUILDERS MUST HAVE A NETWORK.

One of the first activities we do with a new partner is ask them to list all the different ways they network and how they envision themselves sharing the product, hosting classes or events, and building the business. If they look at you with a blank stare, things officially just got challenging. We all network in different ways. Whether it's through our jobs, friends, children, spouses, networking groups, or church, we have a circle of influence. Part of your job may be to help your new builder identify where they network and how they can expand their reach. If your potential builder is stuck at their mom and sister, you may need to reset expectations so you're not setting them up to fail.

RULE #7: YOUR BUILDERS MUST BE COACHABLE.

It's crucial that the people you partner with are willing and open to learn from you and other top leaders. There is no reason to reinvent the wheel. Many MLM masters have shared their secrets through books, training, and coaching. Direct sales companies give builders these resources at low or no cost. If a new builder doesn't show up for business calls and strategy sessions or participate in business-building activities, they're not coachable. I expect every builder to let me coach them; if they don't, they probably should have chosen someone else. Here's a simple test to see how they stack up. Email your new builder step-by-step instructions to get started. In the close, attach a link to your online calendar. Once they have completed the tasks, allow them to schedule a call. Until then, I do not get on a call with them. This not only saves time but also sets expectations. If we're going to work together, I expect you to show up and do what works.

RULE #8: YOUR BUILDERS MUST BE PEOPLE YOU WANT TO PLAY WITH IN TEN YEARS.

It's critical to choose who we work with carefully. I surround myself with successful people, and they provide insight that enables me to succeed. In direct sales, nothing is more important than long-lasting relationships. It's also one of my favorite parts of the business. This industry allows us to connect on a deep level. So the question is, do I want to hang out with you for the next ten years? God willing, my business will be running in ten years. I want builders to become my best friends. I want to spend time together. Travel together. Love their kids.

So I challenge you to look at the builders you're pursuing. Are they motivating you to be the best you can be? Are they pushing you to achieve even more success? Are they pouring value into your life? If not, spend your time and energy on someone else.

"TOO LATE TO JOIN THE BUSINESS?" AND OTHER SALES FAQS

You know how to listen. You know how to sample. You even know how to sell (and to whom). If you're like most women in this industry, you still have questions, concerns, and objections around selling. Any of these common questions running through your head right now?

- "Everybody I know already buys my product from someone else! Am I too late getting into this business?"

- "I'm holding free product workshops, but people don't show up. What am I doing wrong?"

- "My upline helped another person make their first big sales. How do I get them to help me, too?"

- "Selling is *so* hard. How do you keep your confidence up when everybody says no?"

Let's knock out each of these one by one, sister.

"IS IT TOO LATE TO JOIN?"

Think about the last time someone asked what you do. Did the conversation go something like this?

"Hey, Kacie. What are you up to these days? I've been seeing you spending a ton of time volunteering at your kids' schools, traveling, and having fun. I also saw you did a remodel on your house."

"I'm part of a multimillion dollar weight-loss company that is empowering people to take control of their current weight through diet, supplements, and a health plan."

"Oh, really? Is that one of those multilevel marketing companies? You must have been one of the first in the door."

"No, I wasn't. Have you heard of the company?"

"No, I haven't. But I do know that if you don't join in the very beginning, you won't find success."

Interestingly enough, this is a very common misconception in multilevel marketing. The reality is most people have never even heard of your specific product or company. And those who do know the products are a tiny niche within a vast target market. Does it feel like everyone you know already buys your product from someone else? When my builders bring this up, I tell them that it's probably because they're sampling product at yoga studios, nutrition clinics, and herbalist workshops where other like-minded sellers do. Customers who already live the lifestyle you do are "low-hanging fruit." If you always go where your competition goes, you'll compete with them forever. So branch out. Get out a memory jogger and do some searching. Who can your product help that you haven't reached out to? Or even thought of? Are you stuck in your head on who you think the perfect customer is? Have you asked your friends and family who they think would benefit from the product? Or posted a survey on social media? Trust me when I say this. You are never too late to join a network marketing business. You may just need to think outside the box and get creative. Honestly, this is what makes owning your own business fun. You get to choose how things roll. Tap into target markets no else has and you'll make sales no one else can.

"NOBODY'S SHOWING UP!"

I saw a social media post complaining about low event attendance. People are busy. They can't commit to something new in their schedule unless (a) it solves a pain spot, or (b) it's super-duper fun. If your class, workshop, or party isn't both, good luck getting anyone to show.

I challenge struggling builders to get creative with attracting and enticing new people. A friend of mine is a professional chef who offers cooking classes every week all over Park City and Salt Lake City. And every week, she posts pictures of the ten to fifteen paying students who show up. They're having fun. Socializing. Building relationships. People will show up for you, too. Make it clear you're offering something worthwhile.

Remember the three most common complaints? Let people know you're going to help them get started on the path to health, happiness, and financial freedom if they attend your class. Try a workshop title like, "How to Read Makeup Labels and Find the Hidden Toxins." See? Right now you're wondering what harmful chemicals are lurking in your lipstick. That makes two of us . . .

With one headline, you've piqued interest. During the workshop, you can mention all-natural alternatives and talk about how you've built this fun lifestyle around helping people look and feel amazing. Your prize can be samples of the products you talked about in class. Teaching online? Even better. Get attendees' contact information to send their sample, making it easy to follow up with them next week.

"MY UPLINE WON'T HELP ME!"

Did your upline help another builder shatter their income goal, but they don't schedule as many calls with you? Yeah, it happens. If that's your story, take the distance as a compliment. Your upline doesn't see you needing support. You're good, and you're good on your own. It's the people who struggle that need the most help. So if you're not getting equal face time with your upline, chances are it's because you're doing the right money-making activities. You're scheduling your hours, you're talking to five to eight people a week, and you're selling a product, not just sharing it for free. The radio silence isn't intentional.

Still frustrated that your upline plays teacher's pet? Talk to them. Be blunt. Nobody's perfect. It's possible they think you're fine. Voice your concerns. Remind your upline you're committed for the long haul. Chances are they'll provide you the support you need, which is usually a cheerleader to bounce ideas off of.

"HOW DO I STAY CONFIDENT WHEN SALES ARE LOW?"

On a recent coaching call with my upline, I was asked to rate my confidence level. "On a scale of one to ten, ten being the highest, how confident are you in the product? How about in the company? What about your confidence in your ability to hit your sales goals?"

Most people on the call with me answered the first question "ten" without hesitation. The second one, too. But the third one—confidence in our ability—threw most of us for a loop. I'd love to say that everyone on my team steps into their girl power all day, every day. But we all doubt ourselves at some point. When sales slow, self-doubt creeps in and chokes the little confidence we had left.

Instead of thinking about how confident you are, ask yourself how *committed* you are. Are you committed to reaching your sales goals? Are you committed to money-making activities for two consecutive years? Are you committed to creative messaging? Are you committed to expanding your circle of influence and meeting customers your competitors don't even know exist?

If you're nodding along, you're a ten out of ten, sister. You're making things happen. That's what matters. Your confidence will come back when you see your efforts pay off. If, however, you're feeling your commitment settling on one to four, it's only downhill from here. You're going to get weighed down with mom guilt, throw a pity party, and push product on people who don't want it. Whatever sales rank you've earned, you'll stop there, rely on whatever builders you have below you, and sit around collecting your multilevel marketing checks until the amount dwindles. Don't be that girl. Get off your behind and get back to money-making activities. Schedule classes or events. Enroll new builders. Share more product. Do what you know works. Commitment, then confidence. Not the other way around.

CHAPTER 5
SECRETS OF SUCCESSFUL MENTORS

Network marketing is entrepreneurship in a box. Most people who come into this business have no business acumen at all. We're not natural entrepreneurs, and most of us don't have a business degree or sales experience. You could say we don't know what we're doing. And that's OK—nearly everything is set up for us. The brand, the product, the compensation plan, the website content, handouts and brochures, social media templates, and so on. Even the least business-savvy person can succeed, right? There's just one thing missing . . .

Leadership skills. No MLM box comes with them, and it's by far the hardest thing to learn. *Who are you to teach others how to make money? Or lead a team? Or motivate, inspire, and know when to push?* These are valid concerns that constantly muddle our heads as we watch our team grow and seek to advance in business. We look to books and mentors to show us the way, yet most of us fall short. Why? It's simple. If you weren't born with these skills, no one gave them to you, and nobody can teach them, how can you possibly get them?! You, my friend, must learn them yourself.

Every superstar mentor I know learned to lead by screwing up over and over and over. That's the great secret to successful network marketing mentorship—learn from your own silly mistakes. Yes, it sucks, but it's necessary. Imagine you've built your business for two years, following the Five to Eight Rule every week. Now you have one hundred people in your downline. If you're anything like me, you panic. *Nobody ever taught me how to lead a volunteer army!* Yes, that's what you're doing. Leading your team of builders is so different from a typical boss-employee relationship.

As an employee, if you want to keep your job, you do whatever your boss tells you to do. It doesn't matter how you feel about it. Do your job or get fired. That's not how direct sales works. People don't have to work hard to make you rich. Corporate politics, bullying, and intimidation tactics that move employees to action only make builders quit. In the corporate world, everyone's trying to meet someone else's quota. People join MLMs so they can meet their own quota. If your builders wanted a domineering boss, they'd quit this gig and go get one. People want a partner and leader. Yes, they want freedom and control, but they also want to be told exactly what to do. As partners in this industry, we have to find the right balance for our teams.

THE DON'TS OF MENTORSHIP

As a leader of leaders, I did everything wrong so now you don't have to.

DON'T LET YOUR BUILDERS START WITHOUT WHY

When you enroll a new builder, help them get clear on why they're doing this. Knowing what motivates them to build their business changes everything about their outcome. But don't tell them their "why." Ask them.

"Why did you join my team? Do you like this company? What do you want, and what are you willing to do to make it happen?"

Their answers don't have to be complicated. They could be as simple as, "I want a flexible schedule so I can spend more time with my family." A builder's why doesn't have to make them cry. It just has to motivate them beyond belief.

Your builders' why is probably different from yours. That's OK. And what motivates one of your builders may not motivate another. That's OK, too. Unfortunately, what happens a lot in our industry is we treat every builder the same. We want as many people under us as possible, and cookie-cutter mentorship is fast and easy. It also doesn't work. If you help every builder build what *you* want (instead of what *they* want), they won't build anything at all.

And remember, one of the most important things you can do as a leader is to revisit your builders' why. It's common in our industry to get burned out or feel less than motivated. It happens. I recommend scheduling a quarterly review. Spend an hour revisiting your builders' vision board, celebrate their successes, and discuss areas of improvement. Never—I repeat *never*—let your builders lose sight of their mission.

DON'T STOP BUILDING

When I signed up my first builder and took on a mentorship role, I stopped talking to my five to eight new people a week. Dumbest move ever. I went from money-making activities to micromanagement—I stole two hours from my business every day to manage someone else's. All she wanted was to watch what I was doing so she could do it, too. And I stopped doing it.

The best gift you can give your builders is to set an example they can follow. This means doing the work alongside of them. Not everyone is like you and me. We are (or will be) the ultimate network marketing success stories. Remember, most people's financial game changer is an extra $500 to $700 per month. Let your builders know how excited you are to get them there and show them how. Too many leaders look at aspiring side hustlers and think, *Oh my gosh, this is a dream person. They're going to be my top builder and make me millions.* The upline is more excited than the new builder is. Then they set a higher income goal for their builder without including them in it.

Don't be surprised if a new builder gets that first sweet paycheck, then stops building. They don't feel motivated to talk to five to eight new people a *month*, much less a week. All they're willing to do is maintain their rank. That's why you need to step up and keep on obeying the Five to Eight Rule. You're going to meet many aspiring builders who want five hundred extra bucks a month, a few builders who want $5,000 to $7,000 a month, and the one or two unicorns who want $50,000 to $70,000 a month. You don't know who is who yet. I leveled up my financial goal once I reached $5,000 a month in residual income. If you'd asked me when I started if I wanted to become a multimillionaire, I'd have said, "Oh my hell. You're talking to a coal miner's daughter from Wyoming, remember?!" Over time, my motivation as a builder shifted. You never know who else will shift and who won't. It's your responsibility to keep building your business rather than push people beyond what they're willing to do. Accept every builder for the space they're in and what they want to achieve. And make sure you're always walking the walk.

Most builders I rely on choose their paycheck based on their needs and goals. That's good for them and for me. Let your builders upgrade their goals themselves rather than assigning them a number to hit just so you can make your next rank. I always tell my team, "Make sure your expectations align with your builder's goals. If someone's monthly residual income goal is two hundred bucks, set your expectations accordingly. Cheer them on. Celebrate their success when they reach their goal. Who knows? Maybe they'll come to you next month and say, 'You know what? This is fun. I'd like to make two thousand dollars a month.' When you give them your support, they'll see how much you and the team love them. They'll see how amazing this community is. And they'll want to make everyone proud."

DON'T NAG YOUR BUILDERS

Building a network marketing business is all about partnership. When we make our relationship with our builders all about us and our agenda, we screw everything up. Bossing people around motivates no one. It's obvious you're not in this for your builders, you're in it for yourself.

Yes, your builders' success is your success. But if you harp on your builders at the end of the month to sell more when they've already hit their goals, you'll kill their motivation to work hard. They feel pressured to perform. They make bad decisions they normally wouldn't, like spend all their profit on product. They go into next month fried. Guess what? Come the first of the month, you have to talk to these people again. If you squash their enthusiasm, you have to get on the phone and waste time trying to remotivate them. Many people join direct sales because they want to have fun. If your team stops having fun because you're a jerk, expect them to quit. Then block you on social media.

"Why aren't you working harder?" I once asked my team before I knew better. "How are you going to make two thousand dollars in sales in the next forty-eight hours? I need ten of you to put in another two hundred dollar order." Did these orders benefit them? No way. I needed them to sacrifice so I could hit my rank. Talk about selfish. Say stuff like that to your team and you kill everyone's joy. I see other leaders do this all the time. A true leader loves on their people all month long. She motivates builders at the end of the month to hit *their* goals.

One of my leaders called and asked me how to light a fire under her new builder.

"My builder won't do *anything*. It's the last day of the month, she's nowhere near her goal, and she's at her kids' school. She should be teaching oils classes. This *sucks*."

"That's the joy of this business," I said. "She picked this industry so she can be with her kids in the middle of the day. She's prioritized her goals around her family. So no, maybe she's not hitting her business goals. Instead she's hitting her personal goals. Your builders are only going to do what they want and need to do. What has she done this month?"

"Well, she's been online teaching classes and—"

"More classes than you have, I bet. If you're not out there selling product right now, then don't ask her to. Don't expect your team to do anything you're not doing yourself."

"OK, Kacie. I get it. But I'm so far away from hitting my rank it's not even funny."

"Let me tell you a story." I took a deep breath. "In my early days, I got so frustrated. I signed up one of my best girlfriends. I was so desperate to hit my goal that I started questioning everything she was doing. I stopped celebrating her success. It took us two years to repair that friendship. She said to me, 'Kacie, I joined you in this business because I wanted the same freedom you have. You get to pick your kids up from school and go out to dinner with your husband. But at the end of every month, you're just nagging at me to hit a goal. All I want is to pick my kids up from school, too.'" I let that sink in. I could've gone out and enrolled three new customers, put them underneath my team, and we all would've hit our rank. Making someone feel horrible for what they've accomplished is never right. The rank we want our builders to hit doesn't always make a big financial difference for them. Put that pressure on yourself. At the end of the month, it's your business.

I'm leading a volunteer army, and it's my job to celebrate my troops. I don't nag at my builders anymore. It was the most detrimental thing I ever did to my business, and it felt horrible during and after. You want to motivate your team? Love on them. Cheer them on. When they post something on social media, like it. Shoot them a text now and then. *I love what you're doing! You ran a booth at that expo and signed up two new people?! That sounds like an amazing day.* Mentorship is about mutual respect. I wish I hadn't had to learn that the hard way.

DON'T SKIP CRUCIAL CONVERSATIONS

How do you motivate people? What do you say to somebody who's feeling stuck? What do you do when a builder just doesn't feel like building?

If you're like most leaders, you talk about everything that's *not* happening in their business, which they already know. My builders know when they're falling behind. They don't need me calling them up saying, "Well, how many events have you had? Do more." That's what makes people say, "This isn't for me. I'm so stressed out. I can't do this." So stupid. As women, we already tend to focus on the bad. Trust me, your builder is already thinking, *Oh my gosh, I had an event, and no one showed up. I must be terrible at this. There is no hope for me.* Don't pile onto that negativity.

If you want to keep people in this business and help them succeed, tell them what they're doing *right* so they can do more of it. When one of my builders gets stuck, I ask them to draw two perpendicular lines, creating four boxes on a piece of paper. Then I have them write their answers to these questions, one answer for each box:

- What is working?

- What do you enjoy?

- What is sucking?

- What do you hate?

When you take your team through this exercise, ask more questions to help them get clear on the right next steps.

"I really love sharing this product," your builder might say. "I love getting text messages from a new customer who loves how her skin looks. What works for me is every Monday, Tuesday, and Wednesday when I work eight to noon. And I hate doing live video on social media. I keep trying, but every time I get on there, I get anxiety for the next four hours."

"OK," you say. "How do we get rid of these things you hate and next month implement more of what you love?"

If your builders do what they enjoy, they'll stick around, and they'll bring in more volume. All because of one crucial conversation.

When your builders ask for advice, don't tell them what they should do. Tell them what *you* did.

One of my builders said to me, "I don't know how to invite people to an event. I keep teaching them, but I can't get anyone to show up. Is something wrong with my message?"

I seized that coaching opportunity.

"We've all been there." I said, "Let's find out everything we can about getting people to show up. For starters, I used to hold events where no one showed up. You know what I did? I found a consistent place to host every single week, and if people didn't show up, I still went. I spent the hour doing work I needed to be doing anyway, and eventually, people started coming. For me, that consistency worked. Let's get on a call with the team and see what other people have done to increase their turnout."

Celebrate success. Let your builders identify what's not working. And inspire them to do the right thing on their terms. This is leadership. You're not telling your team what to do; you're helping them find their own answers. Remember— mentor, not boss.

DON'T BE A COUNSELOR

I don't know about you, but I didn't sign up to be a therapist when I started my networking marketing business. Set up boundaries so you don't have to be one either. If a team member wants a spot on your calendar, make sure it's during your work hours. When you talk, keep things professional. I'm not heartless—I love talking about kids and husbands and trips. But we have to honor the fact that we're running a business. Would you go into your boss's office and ask for personal advice on your divorce? No, you'd say, "Hey, want to go get a glass of wine with me after work? I really need some girl time."

Honor your and your team's time. If you're there to mentor, great. If you're there to be a friend, that's great, too—but don't be one during business hours.

DON'T WING IT

Every meeting with my team is focused. We don't just show up to see what happens. Before my weekly check-in call, I send a questionnaire to each builder. This simple form lets everyone tell me where they're stuck, what they need, and how they expect me to help. The same questions every week help maintain a structured, productive environment.

SAMPLE WEEKLY BUILDER CHECK-IN PRE-MEETING QUESTIONNAIRE

1. On a scale of 1–10, how are you feeling about your business right now? (1 = It's been a challenging week! 10 = I'm in LOVE with this business.)

2. What worked well in your business this past week? What are you celebrating?

3. What do you feel is your biggest obstacle right now?

4. What are you doing to address it?

5. What is your goal this week? Or what would you like to accomplish?

6. What vital steps are needed to move forward to reach your goal for this week?

7. How is the morale on your team? What support do they need?

8. Any additional questions you have for me?

9. Is there a concern that you need to speak with me about personally? If so, let's set up a time to talk.

DON'T ASK YOUR BUILDERS TO BE SOMEONE ELSE

Everyone who starts a business in network marketing should take the StrengthsFinder assessment by Tom Rath and share their results with their upline. The assessment helps a new builder and their leader figure out the most effective way to build the business in alignment with the builder's strengths. Everyone's strengths are different. For me, I'm all about loving on people and keeping a peaceful environment. My husband loves to have fun. When we host a party, he entertains everyone because that's what he's good at. When a family friend goes through a tough time, I invite them over for a heart-to-heart because I know how to help others feel safe and loved. Bring your genuine self into your business—build on your own strengths.

Expect the same from your builders. Ask them what they're willing to do with their strengths. Say you shine when you're in the spotlight. Are you willing to take thousands of selfies and show up on social media forever? Maybe you love to travel. Willing to be a globe-trotter on the road twenty-four days a month? Whatever your strengths are, put them to good use.

For example, my StrengthsFinder results tell me I'm futuristic. So I'm constantly working out my future. Every plan I make revolves around where I want to go. I'm also energized by getting things done and being thoughtful about it. My eye for plans means I am at my best when I'm gathering information, resources, or other people's strengths to serve a greater purpose. My purpose is to help other women find theirs. My builders rely on me for this inspiration and all the overwhelming information I'm able to collect and summarize in bite-size bits.

What do all of my plans have in common? I'm fueled by a desire to have an impact. That's why I feel energized as I learn. I know the information and resources I come across will help me help more women on a massive scale without giving up who I am. I only have so much time like everyone else. It's no wonder I want my builders to be cooler than me. Because I *need* them to be.

My deep certainty in what I stand for—another strength— means people value my word long before I sell them a product. So when I do make an offer, they invest without thinking twice. They know that whatever I recommend is worth it because I've already tried and tested it.

See how my strengths play well with my network marketing business? Why would I try to be who I am not? Just as I know what I have a knack for in this business, I'm also aware of what I should avoid. For example, because I plan for the future, I have a tendency to consult the past. I'm better off staying away from trying to find value in things that went wrong in my life. It's not productive. I feel drained. Miserable. Sad. And it takes far too long to get my energy flowing again toward the greatness I want to create in my future. For me, taking a couple of minutes every day to visualize everything going perfectly gets me what I want. The right thoughts inspire the right action.

This is true for you as well. So what are your strengths? What should you build your business on? No two successful networking marketing businesses are the same, and that's how it should be. A business is only as strong as its owner, and you, friend, are already stronger than you know.

DON'T FORGET WHY YOU ARE DOING THIS

I was in Hawaii. America's de facto tropical paradise. All the top performers at my company gathered for a special week of celebrating and socializing. My fellow superstars planned to spend the week sunbathing, sightseeing, and brainstorming ideas. Sounds amazing, doesn't it? Yet I was miserable. Flustered. Antsy. I was afraid I'd lost my passion for the business. I needed to do something more. I didn't feel like I was fulfilling my big picture. I felt stuck. Complacent. Comfortable. Yes, I'd set goals and achieved them. The paychecks I got and the people I worked with were amazing. So why didn't I look forward to lounging by the waves with like-minded women?

Our first day in Hawaii kicked off with a welcome event and an amazing drive to a private beach and energizing hike. Next to me happened to be a founding executive of my business. My heart skipped. Everyone in the company knows that when you say something to this lady, you'd better have your ducks in a row because she's going to challenge you, push you outside of your comfort zone, and hold you accountable for blowing past whatever has you stuck. In hindsight, I'm sure it was *not* a coincidence I sat next to her.

I reeled in my inner fangirl and started talking. I needed genuine advice. *Who in their right mind tells a company executive they lack motivation and lost their business mojo?* I made a split-second decision—to be honest with her. I took a deep breath and told her everything I'm telling you now.

"I don't know what my 'why' is anymore. I make a ton of money. I'm financially free. I've got more free time than anyone I know. I've helped thousands upon thousands upon thousands of women become successful. Five years ago, *that* was my why. I still want to empower women. That's still part of the big picture, but I'm lost. What am I supposed to do now?"

She smiled. "Let me ask you something. What do you love most about this company? What made you commit to this company in the first place?"

"The products," I said. "I've always loved what the products do for families." I paused.

I realized something in that moment—I wasn't acting on my whole passion anymore. Sure, I loved empowering other women in the business, but that was my only focus. I wasn't helping people in *all* realms of life. I wasn't bringing in equal amounts of customers, sharers, and business builders. That's the sweet spot in this business. Think about it for a second. Most people join a network marketing company for product discounts. They start as a customer. Then they fall in love and start talking. They become sharers. They begin to dream of your lifestyle. Then they become your partner. I forgot the process that once brought me so much joy. The growth. The excitement. The challenge. All the things that make network marketing so awesome.

For the first time in months, I felt pumped to get back to what made my heart sing. I was back on track and ready to empower women in every way. I was ready to serve every single woman who entered my life on the level that *they* desired. I was no longer seeking one specific individual to empower. I was ready to change the world and share with anyone who would listen.

CHAPTER 6

NETWORK MARKETING ONLINE

Every network marketer wants to grow their online presence. Why wouldn't they? When you bring your business online, you can reach millions of people. Get your message out there the right way and you can connect with your five to eight new people by Monday morning at 8:00.

The problem is, most network marketers do the whole online thing *all wrong*. Their practices ensure that no one will ever join their team, buy from them, or refer a friend who would. You probably know what "all wrong" looks like, right? I'm talking about the people who blow up your news feeds, spam your in-box, and turn everyone off from multilevel marketing. Remember that friend from college who joined an MLM and wouldn't stop inviting you to online "parties"? Every day, she clogged your news feed with posts about her business—until finally you had enough and clicked "unfollow" (or even "unfriend"). Or maybe it wasn't a friend who spammed the crap out of you. Just this weekend, I got a message from a gal selling skin-care cream.

Hey, Kacie. It was so amazing to connect with you. I'm so glad we had that great conversation. If you go to my site and place your first order, I'll send you a free sunscreen.

Her name didn't sound familiar. I ran through the last week in my head. Nope, I definitely hadn't talked to anyone about skin care. Not in person, not online, not anywhere.

What conversation? I don't even know you, I responded. *And I'm certain we did not connect.*

I didn't wait to see what her follow-up would be. Her dishonesty ruined any chance of ever selling me anything. I clicked "block" and got on with my day.

Since you're reading this book, I know you believe network marketing is an awesome industry. But if you're sending random messages to people like skin-care girl, you're not helping anyone, and you're definitely not selling anything. No wonder people give us a hard time. When people pick on business owners, it's always us network marketers. We do the dumbest stuff online. We push product on people who don't want it. We reach out to family and friends' contacts. We invade social media groups and spam someone else's tribe. We invite all our connections to parties so we can beg them to buy skin care, leggings, oils, whatever. I can't tell you how many times

I've wanted to message someone and blow them out of the water. *Pull your head out of the sand and get some common courtesy.* It's not proper etiquette on social media to lie to strangers. It's not good to lie to anyone ever. So if we didn't connect, let's not pretend we did. And you're not welcome to invade my friends list. They're my friends. Go make your own.

OK. That's my rant. I get it. These women are excited about their product, their business, and their new opportunity. But we can't just go straight for the sale. When we've exhausted our family and friends begging for sales, we can't instaspam people with links to "buy now." That's not how network marketing online works. That's not how anything works. This is a relationship business. Think about it. You don't go into a cocktail party and start selling to people. "Hey, I've got a product, you want to buy it?" You get to know each other first. Maybe you like each other and you build up trust. You tell them your story. They tell you about their kids. Then and only then do you say, "Hey, can I get your business card?" or "Hey, let's do lunch." It's the same when you market on the internet. People want to buy from those they know, like, and trust.

"But Kacie, how do I do that online? It's not like we're talking face-to-face." You'd be surprised how often our fellow network marketers ask me this. Let me answer that question once and for all.

MY BEST ONLINE MARKETING TIP: TARGET THE PERFECT CUSTOMER

When you market online, market to one person. Just one. Not everyone with a credit card. Not everyone on your friends list or in your contacts. One. Person. This person should be your ideal customer. The one who clicks with you and what you're selling. The one you see becoming a customer, then a sharer, and maybe even a builder—your ideal partner in this business.

Ask any successful MLM business builder and they'll tell you that in the beginning, they enrolled anyone who was breathing. They didn't care *who* bought, just *that* they bought. "Oh, you have skin? You need my skin-care line." Then we realized something—if we market to everyone, we're bouncing back and forth between leads like a ping-pong ball. We're distracted. Try to serve everyone, and we serve no one. That's not the approach we take anymore. We've evolved our messaging to target the specific individual who we want to work with.

Whenever I enroll a new builder, I walk them through an avatar exercise. *A what? That movie with those blue people?* No, "avatar" is internet guruspeak for your perfect customer. Your ideal partner. If you have a copy of *The Essential Planner*, flip open and complete this activity now. It's simple. In the avatar exercise, I help you get clear on two things: demographics and psychographics. The demographics we care about are:

- Age
- Sex

- Location

- Education

- Current career/income

- Lifestyle

Psychographics to identify are:

- Personality

- Values

- Opinions

- Attitude

- Interests

- Pain points

For online marketers, the most important psychographic is the last one—pain points. What does your ideal client struggle with, and what are they willing to do to fix it? Put your psychographics and demographics together and you have a three-dimensional person. For example, my perfect customer is an educated female ages thirty-five to fifty-five in the United States. She desires financial freedom for herself and her family, but she's not desperate for extra cash. This woman is a lifelong learner, she's coachable, she's driven, and she's open to opportunity—and to alternative medicine. Her pain point is that she doesn't feel like she has permission to have something of her own.

So how do you decide this stuff? How do you pick who you want your avatar to be? Well, you don't. You look at who you're already attracting. That's what I did, and I realized my customers had eerily similar demographics and psychographics in common.

Once you know what your best customers, raving fan sharers, and rock star builders have in common, combine those traits into one person, your avatar. Then think about somebody you know who fits this description—a friend, a colleague, a mentor—and use their image to put a face to your avatar. Now whenever you type, post, or send anything as you market your business online, imagine you're typing, posting, and sending only to them. In other words, you're creating content to educate your perfect customer about your product and your opportunity while they get to know, like, and trust you. Most of the time, people are interested in the product you have to sell—as long as you market your business in a non-salesy way. How do you do that? Simple. Tell your story. Be authentic. Show your perfect customer you're just like her. And if you're not, find commonalities or ways to connect (or rethink your avatar).

If your ideal customer is an athlete, make everything you say about your business relate to fitness or sports. Athletes are competitive, so you can create content about how your product can give performers an incredible edge. What you don't want to do is talk about the diaper bag you bought this weekend. How are you going to get a following of athletes if you're talking about basketball here and biodegradable diapers there? Neither athletes nor parents will feel like you're speaking to them. You'll lose everyone's attention. Now, if you want to attract new moms, talk about using your product with babies. Who wants to follow content like that? You guessed it—moms. If that's your ideal customer, you're doing online marketing right.

Whatever you do, don't skip this avatar exercise. If you don't know who you're talking to, you'll end up doing what so many inexperienced network marketers do. They see a successful leader post a powerful, deeply personal article on social media, then they copy the whole freaking post and put it on their own page. Then their friends see it and copy it, too. Next thing you know, the same plagiarized post shows up forty-five times in the original poster's news feed. Guess what, sister? That *won't* make her happy.

If you know who your perfect customer is, you'll know exactly what to say. You won't have to rip off anyone else's content and claim it as your own. You'll be laser focused. *This is who I'm marketing to, so this is the information they need, and this is how I get it to them.* If you copy what someone else is doing, you're mixing messages and audiences. Their ideal client? Probably not yours. Remember, you're not here for everyone. You're just speaking to one person.

You're probably wondering what I mean by content and information. What type of content? Articles? Videos? And how do you educate people about your product without getting blocked? All good questions with great answers. Buckle your learning seat belt, sister, because this information-packed idea coaster is about to take off.

THE ONLY MARKETING PLAN YOU'LL EVER NEED

So you're ready to attract your perfect customer with your consistent, subtle, cool messaging. Great. You open a blank document. You start typing. Whatever pops into your head becomes an article. You publish it on social media and your blog, then email it to your contacts. Two or three weeks go by, and you realize your people haven't heard from you in a while. You have no idea what to say next because you stuffed all your good ideas into that first article.

Sister, I have the cure for this one-and-done problem. You're never going to get stuck coming up with content ideas *again*. Coming up with ideas for articles, emails, social media posts, and videos is easy when you're not starting from scratch. I write about three kinds of topics:

- an educational topic

- a behind-the-scenes topic

- a get-to-know-me topic

I start by picking a topic and brainstorming several pieces of content. For example, January is all about new beginnings. So I post on how to use your copy of *The Essential Planner*. I teach you how to get self-motivated and set goals. I'm sharing tips about oils of inspiration. Every month, I switch up the topic so I'm not showing my audience the same thing over and over. So

February might be about my morning meditation, and March could be a customer testimonial. You can also follow what your company is doing. Any promotions, special events, or new product releases scheduled? Prepare your content calendar accordingly. The easiest way to keep track of your content ideas is to type them into a simple spreadsheet. Nobody wants to try to remember what they talked about three months ago!

Which content ideas should you turn into articles, emails, and videos? How often should you post that content and where? Don't worry, I'm going to cover all that. First, I'm going to teach you the nuances of each medium (e.g., blog, email, social media, video, etc.) and how to approach each for maximum results.

BLOGGING 101

When you brain dump ideas into your spreadsheet, the first piece of content you'll want to create is an article. Either you write it yourself or make some notes, talk through them, and hire someone to transcribe and edit your recording (like I do). You could post this article on social media, but it's better to publish on a platform you own and manage—your blog, which appears on your website (more on that in a minute). Since social media companies are changing rules and banning people left and right, you don't want to risk losing your work. Plus, when you post on your blog, you get to take advantage of search engine optimization (SEO), which is all about increasing the quantity and quality of new website visitors. Search engines like

Google *love* websites with consistent long-form content. That means over time, your website moves higher and higher up in internet search rankings so even more people can find you and your business.

Why *long-form* content? Because many network marketing newbies write a 300-word paragraph and call it an article. That's not how this works. Long-form content is "in" right now. That's 1,000 to 1,500 words per article. Google wants to promote websites with rich, impactful content, and that won't be you if your articles aren't much longer than a tweet. That said, don't feel like you have to write a new novella every month to keep up with your blog. All I do is pick two content ideas from my spreadsheet every month, write one article about each, and publish the articles on my blog (and cross-post the links to social media). Now, if you're an avid writer, I would never tell you *not* to blog a few times a week. For most of us, two articles a month is about all we can handle. I recommend putting a recurring event or reminder on your digital calendar or in your planner so you never forget to publish your blogs.

If that still seems like too much to wrap your head around, cut it back to just one a month. Consistency is more important than quantity. Once you've been at it for a while, you'll get more confident and you can bump things up. If you notice that your creativity flows in "bursts," try knocking out a few articles in one sitting. Save them, and then all you have to do is copy and paste when posting time rolls around.

WEBSITES 101

I'm not talking about your company's website. In my case, that's the corporate essential oil brand. Yes, you probably need your own separate website. A website is not essential if you're a sharer, new builder, or experienced builder with a vast off-line following. If you want to build this business online, though, I can't see how you'd do so without your own website.

But Kacie, what if I don't know how to code? I don't know the first thing about how to design or manage a website. Isn't it hard?!

Breathe. One question at a time. Why your own site? Because there are thousands of other direct sales representatives out there with their own websites, and you want people placing orders through you. Having your own website also creates your own brand identity. If your family relies on your MLM business for income, what happens if the parent company closes? You have nothing. But if you build your own brand outside of the company, you have something you can expand, a message that speaks to your ideal customer. Fortunately, building and maintaining a website won't be hard after you finish reading this section.

First, what do you put on your site? A good website shares who you are, how you solve your ideal customer's problem, and what makes your solution different (your home page); tells your story (your about page); lets customers and sharers order product (your shop); allows future builders to contact you about enrolling (contact page); and features your blog articles (blog). Five pages total. Pretty straightforward.

WEBSITE STARTER CHECKLIST

Now that I've got you excited to build your website, let's go over the simple steps to launch it:

1. Decide what domain name to use. (I use my business name, but your personal name is an awesome place to start if you don't have a business name registered with your state yet.)

2. Buy your domain from a domain registry. (I use GoDaddy, but there are tons of other places like Bluehost and Namecheap.)

3. Choose a website host (I use SiteGround for this.)

4. Choose a content management system (CMS) to build your site. I use WordPress. Download the CMS to your website via your host provider. (Check with your host on how best to do this.)

5. Pick a website theme and customize with your own images and text. I use a WordPress theme called Divi, which is basically a website template I can play around with making images and texts look exactly how I want. If you want to keep your website to a simple blog, you don't have to get all fancy. A free WordPress theme is all you need.

Now, I'm no website designer, but I'll let you in on a little hack to come up with an appealing site design—consult yourself. What do you like about the look and feel of the websites you have bookmarked? Never thought about it? That's OK. Take a moment now and go to three of your favorite websites. What do you notice about them? What do you like? What do you dislike? For me, I like simple designs that are aesthetically pleasing. For example, I don't like "busy," so I love a plain white background. I like it when all text is easy to read. Tons of images and videos don't clutter the flow of the home page. I found a few websites that clicked with me, and I "borrowed" design elements from each of them to build my own website. Check me out at www.KacieVaudrey.com, leave a comment, and tell me what you think. If you love my site as much as I do, borrow my layout. This is the only time it's OK to "steal."

THE OFFER BEFORE THE OFFER

When people visit your home page, the first thing they should see on your site is an opt-in form to type their email address into. Why would anyone do this? Simple—you have something they want, and they have to give you their email to get it. In return for subscribing to your emails, they'll receive something exciting and exclusive they can't get anywhere else. To get people to opt in for my emails, I created seasonal essential oils recipe ebooks, diffuser blend guides, and essential oil first aid kit checklists. I've found that my perfect customer *loves* ebooks. When you're selling a product, people want to know how to use it. If you can provide a visually appealing, easy-to-use ebook so subscribers can learn how to use your product *before* they buy it, you're going to get people on your list—and many of them will buy from you.

What if you have an opt-in form with the alluring offer you created, but nobody opts in? If you get little web traffic because you're new to the game, advertise your opt-in freebie on social media. Feature a beautiful picture of your recipe ebook, guide, or checklist in the ad, and keep your call-to-action simple. "Download now." People click the link in your post, which takes them to your website's opt-in form. Be careful not to mention your business opportunity in your post. Social media companies may shut you down if you run an ad that talks about joining your network marketing team. Until this unofficial rule changes, focus on educating new and future customers about your product through free content they can only get when they join your list. And when you send out those two newsletters every month (more on this next), invite them to buy your product or join your team. The larger your list, the more people will say yes.

EMAIL MARKETING 101

Now you have your website, you're writing blog articles, and you're gaining subscribers who you can send emails to. What do you send them? Repurpose those articles. If you're publishing two blog articles a month, how many emails are you sending? That's right, two newsletters per month. As with all things online marketing, the more you can do, the better. But *only* if what you're doing is working for you. What I'm teaching you now are online marketing best practices. That said, the one and *only* point of marketing is to help you find new people every week and to systematize follow-up. So if sending forty-five emails a week keeps you so busy you don't get around to meeting five to eight new people, don't send the emails. Meeting your five to eight new people is your priority. Try to send at least two emails a month. If your schedule can't handle any more than that, that's OK.

I'm a big fan of trying to get anybody and everybody on my email list versus only depending on social media. If (or when) a social media channel shuts us down for some arbitrary reason, my email list is my saving grace. At my company, we have our own back office email marketing platform, but not every MLM entrepreneur is so fortunate. When I started my business, I saw reps from other companies bcc'ing every email address in their contacts (including me). That's a great way to get caught by every spam filter on the planet. Never, ever send your business email from your personal email account (Gmail, Yahoo, etc.). Use a professional email address. A professional email address from G Suite for only five dollars per month is a great option. Meanwhile, use a free or low-cost email marketing platform like Mailchimp to build your email subscriber list.

What are subscribers, you ask? They're people who give you permission to send them marketing emails. How do they give you their permission? They type their email into your website opt-in form.

SOCIAL MEDIA 101

On social media, consistency beats trendy. Consistency beats pretty. Consistency even beats *perfect*. The point of online marketing is to get your business in front of people so they follow you, engage with you, and then buy from you. If you're only posting here and there, and your content is all over the place, people aren't going to follow you—even if you have a killer product.

Marketing experts say if you want someone to buy from you, you need to "touch" them twenty times.[1] In online marketing, that means they have to have twenty interactions with your brand. They could see your post, visit your blog, open your email, and watch your live video. I'm not saying you should try to blow up every social media channel at once. You'll drive yourself crazy trying to keep up with all the posts, and your engagement will be sporadic at best. Consistency, remember? That's our key. The good news is, affordable social media tools like Hootsuite, Later, MeetEdgar, and Social Bee let you schedule posts to publish at a later date. That means you can knock out all your posts for the whole week in one hour on Monday morning. If you're going to show up every day on Facebook, you can use their native future posting option to schedule content for a future date.

Now, which platform is best? That depends on where your avatar is hanging out. Not everyone is on Facebook. Not everyone is on Instagram or Pinterest. Your ideal customers could be on Twitter. It all depends on who you want to reach.

That's why it's important to know who your perfect customer is. If she's looking for recipes online, you'll want to focus on Pinterest. Or does she want to find an online community and connect with like-minded people? Better show up on Facebook. Does she like to apply flattering filters to all her selfies? She's probably on Instagram, so you should be, too.

Once you identify which social media channel or channels your perfect customer spends time on, start showing up there. That doesn't mean you post product links eight times an hour. Who wants to be flooded with promotions? We get enough ads in our news feed as it is. Nobody on social media says to themselves, *I love following accounts that are always posting pictures of a new product with a link to go buy it for 10 percent off.*

It's OK to let people know what you do. In fact, it's essential. "I sell leggings, come buy from me," is not a winning message. If you go to my personal social media pages, the only place you'll see my company mentioned is my bio. But you do know what I'm all about. My business is now in the back of your head. So who are you going to call when your kiddo has a headache, your partner gets sick, or your skin flares up? The lady with a solution for everything—me.

If I used my whole profile space to talk about my business, what impression would that give you? *Geez, this lady is pushy. Maybe she sells a good product, but it's not worth buying if it means I have to talk to her.* That's the last thing you want people thinking. Instead, you want to show that you're easy-going, approachable, and not at all salesy. Then you know what people will think? *Wow, look at this woman's life. She seems so kind and genuine. And she sells the best cleaning products on the market. I keep thinking about trying those, but I don't know where to start. I bet she'd answer my questions.* That's the beauty of being subtle with your online marketing. So how can you be subtle while drawing people to your business?

First of all, don't blend in. Posting a photo of an eye shadow palette or an inspirational quote meme doesn't create any customers. That's not marketing. That's boring. If you want to get customers using social media, stand out. Be interesting. Enticing. *Cool.* Incorporate your product into real life. Post pictures and videos that make people go, *Wow, I want that lifestyle, too.* Let your posts reflect who you are and why your life is so incredibly fun.

I post photos of me spraying homemade bug spray on my horses and dropping oregano into the chickens' water to fight infection. I'm not pushing my product on people; I'm proving I believe in my products. I use them myself. What I'm not posting are Friday night party pics. If I go out with some girlfriends and get a little tipsy, I'm not going to post a photo captioned, *Woohoo! Wild Friday night with my girls!* I don't care who your perfect customer is, I'm sure that's not what they want to see. Instead, I might post a photo of a glass of wine captioned, *Enjoying a glass of wine and some girl talk with my bestie #lifeisgood.* I'm not being fake—I'm living the lifestyle people think I live, and that includes indulging once in a while. That's how you show up as authentic and interesting on social media. Bring a little joy to your audience's lives when you post. Isn't that why we check social media eighty times a day? For an inspirational pick-me-up? A meme that makes us literally LOL? A little hope and some motivation? *Yeah, that's really cool. I should put my phone down and go build an awesome life.*

Want more examples of what consistent, subtle, and cool look like in action? Find ten people to follow—entrepreneurs, celebrities, influencers—who target the same perfect customer you do. For me, I love Reese Witherspoon and her book club. So do many of my customers, sharers, and builders. Every post invites women to join the conversation, and every image she posts is beautiful.

Who is your Reese Witherspoon? Watch how they market themselves on social media. Now, don't go swiping their stuff. No copying. Watch their posts to get ideas. What kind of content gets a lot of engagement with their followers? What are their followers buying into already? After all, you're trying to reach the same people. Take the inspiration these ten accounts give you and use it to post similar messages about your own lifestyle and products.

One more thing. Whatever you do, no comparing. I always say comparison is the thief of all joy. Nobody needs that kind of negativity in their life. Don't compare your whole story to someone else's highlights reel.

ARE GROUPS ALL THAT?

I've created a free social media group for my builders, sharers, and customers. It's an active, engaged community where members get to interact with me and each other while receiving exclusive education. Anytime I post in the group, my tribe blows up the post with likes, comments, and replies. It's crazy how much fun we have in there.

My group isn't huge because I keep it closed. You can't join unless you're already on my team or you've already bought a product from me. But I have opened my group up to all my builders, their builders, their builders' builders, and so on, so they don't have to start and manage their own groups. It's a relief to have one community where everyone can go to hang out and support each other.

If you love the idea of building an online community to supplement real-life relationships, you can start a private group or build a public one and invite whoever. If you go public, people can find you from a keyword search based on your business or industry. When you start your group, be proactive about building membership. Anytime you post a live video, publish a blog post, or send an email, close with a call to action to join your free community group.

Like my articles and emails, the content in my group follows a pattern. I do Motivation Mondays, Tuesday Tips, Wednesday Wisdom, Throwback Thursdays (sometimes Thoughtful Thursdays or Thankful Thursdays), and Feel Good

Fridays. Every day, I post a short paragraph with an image or video according to the theme. Themes make it easy to create quality content that keeps people coming back. Plus, it's the closest thing to content creation on autopilot. I gather my ideas, posts, and images in a folder months in advance so I just grab and go for the day. If I've got a lesson or story to share that doesn't relate to the day's theme, that's fine. If I have something to say, I don't wait until the right day. I say what I have to say and grab an idea from my folder the next day. Just like with email, if a social media group sounds like too much of a time killer or it's just not your thing, focus on other ways in this chapter to meet your five to eight new people a week.

VIDEO MARKETING 101

Video is one hundred times more likely to create that know, like, and trust factor than any other medium. Few people are comfortable on camera. Is that you? No judgment from me, sister. You have to figure out what works best for you. For me, I say the sweaty palms are worth it.

If you want to try it, keep your videos three to five minutes long, and always end on a call to action. Aside from that, there is no right or wrong way to do a video. I like to work from a script (like one of my articles), but impromptu videos get the best results. One thing you don't have to worry about is messing up. Fumble a word? That's OK. Bad hair day? Even better. People share my videos like crazy when I show up as the real me in all my authenticity. In one four-minute video I did, I'm sitting in a chair out in my barn. One of our horses snuck up behind me and started nibbling my hair. I spun around and swatted Dually, then panicked and started petting him. When I stopped the recording I thought, *Oh my God, this is so terrible.* But I had to get ready for my team call, so I didn't redo it. I posted it anyway, and the video has over ten thousand views.

If you take one thing away from this chapter, I hope it's this: whatever online marketing tools you use, stay true to yourself while you're using them. The more natural you feel on the page, in a post, or on camera, the more people will stop what they're doing and pay attention to you. Don't try to be someone you're not. After all, everyone else is already taken. If more people took that advice to heart, we'd all be a lot happier. And who knows? If just one woman sees you being your proud, authentic self, maybe she'll feel inspired to be herself, too.

CHAPTER 7

BUTTERFLIES EVERY DAY

You picked up this book because you're tired of the boring status quo way of earning income. Now you're seeing yourself living that dream. Not the one with the yachts—the one where you get to design your schedule, choose your paycheck, and spend more time with the people you love. Because when you're surrounded by authentic women who focus on the people and the product over the profit, everything flows— including the profit.

No other product, business model, or industry offers that. In no other industry do women get to choose how we work, when we work, and why we work. Network marketing means freedom. It means empowerment. It means the lifestyle you desire. It means the attention your family needs. It means so much free time that you feel like a little kid again. *What amazing things are going to happen today?*

Whatever success looks like to you, this industry can give it to you. I tell every builder this, whether they've been in direct sales their entire adult life or they're just now learning there is an alternative to the cubicle. I love watching women grow, set goals, and achieve them. I've helped women change careers, even get a career for the first time after being a stay-at-home mom for years. Their love for growing this business is over-the-top amazing. And I get to be that person who gently pushes them out of their comfort zone . . . while also acting as the reality police. I hope this book has been exactly that for you, too.

A few months ago, someone on my team got this insane idea to blitz every email address in her contacts with a product promotion. No introductions, no context. Just the pitch. I could see the dollar signs in her eyes.

"Listen," I told her. "If the money seems too good to be true, it probably is. Is that how you want to feed your family? With a pushy sales pitch? Let's step back and do what we know works. We build relationships. We create trust. And we never, *ever* back people into a corner and scare them into buying something they don't want."

I saw her switch flip. She never sent the email blast. The week I wrote this chapter, she achieved her $2,000 per month goal. All because she followed a system and stuck to our ethics.

Follow the system in this book and your paychecks will come, too. So will the food in the fridge, the gas in the tank, and even the tropical beach vacations. They will. No matter what. Until they do, you must have faith. Trust the process. Stick to the plan. Schedule those money-making activities. Love on your circle of influence. Celebrate your builders' success. Stay true to you. As long as you're loving people and changing lives daily, you'll have butterflies in your stomach every morning. You'll wake up thinking, *Yeah ... I'll be doing this forever.*

ACKNOWLEDGMENTS

Without my family, my friends, or my team, I doubt this book would've happened. So you have them to thank . . . or blame. Your call.

I want to thank first and foremost my parents for supporting me in this journey. You gave me my work ethic. You taught me how to commit. And you stuck by me when I forgot. Thank you for inspiring me to always try new adventures.

My husband, Mike, has been my number one cheerleader. You share the company and the product with everyone. Everywhere I go, I'm constantly hearing about how you're bragging about me. I so appreciate your excitement about this business.

Thank you to all of my kiddos. Emma, thank you for listening to me talk about the book. You're the best at bouncing ideas off of. Sulli, I'm so grateful that you asked me every single day if the book was done. You've kept me going.

Thank you to Mike's daughters. I'm grateful for your trust in me in this life. Thank you for accepting me as a bonus mom. Katie (Kenny), thank you for bringing amazing grandbabies into my life. They're such a great distraction from work. You've taught me a lot about persistence till the end. The twins, Hannah and Brynne, I love being around you. You've supported me through this entire journey. Plus, you're hilarious. You know what I'm talking about. Megan, I appreciate all the times you've helped me to see the color in life. Things aren't always as they seem, and that's OK.

To my team, I say thank you. You've taught me so much about who I am. You've stuck it out with me as I did amazing things and really bad things. We've figured out this industry together.

I'm grateful for my front-line leaders, my builders, who've endured this adventure with me.

Thank you to my cross-line leaders, who teach me something new every day.

To the coaches in my life, thank you. You've taught me how to soul-search and find soul answers. You've pushed me to the next level of professionalism and expertise. I wouldn't be here without all of you.

Thank you Dawn for being an amazing business manager. Not only do you keep me on track and provide gorgeous content for the world to enjoy, you allow me to be my best visionary self while you do your best work in execution.

And thank you Joshua for helping me write this book. This process was unlike anything I've ever done in my life. Thank you for seeing me through to the end.

NOTES

Chapter 1

1. Fiona Simpson, "Home Is Where The Work Is: The Rise of Home-Based Franchises," *Forbes*, December 10, 2018, https://www.forbes.com/sites/fionasimpson1/2018/11/26/home-is-where-the-work-is-the-rise-of-home-based-franchises/#17734e364196.
2. "Direct Selling in the United States: 2017 Facts and Data." Direct Selling Association, 2018, accessed November 19, 2019, https://www.dsa.org/docs/default-source/research/dsa_2017_factsanddata_2018.pdf.

Chapter 3

1. John Call, "Multitasking—Efficient or a Waste of Time?" *Psychology Today*, December 26, 2008, https://www.psychologytoday.com/us/blog/crisis-center/200809/multitasking-efficient-or-waste-time.

Chapter 4

1. Chris Orlob, "Who's Better at Selling: Men or Women? Data from 30,469 Sales Calls," *HubSpot* (blog), accessed November 19, 2019, https://blog.hubspot.com/sales/men-vs-women-selling.

Chapter 6

1. Jeffry Pilcher, "Say It Again: Messages Are More Effective When Repeated," The Financial Brand, November 15, 2018, https://thefinancialbrand.com/42323/advertising-marketing-messages-effective-frequency/.

ABOUT THE AUTHOR

Kacie Vaudrey is an author, coach, and entrepreneur serving over 110,000 women on their journey to find their purpose, passion, and sweet spot. As a successful network marketer, Kacie helps women create an intentional lifestyle around their goals and desires. Her first book, *The Essentials: Everything Women Need to Know to Make It as a Network Marketer*, and its companion *The Essential Planner: The Only Self-Care Planner & Network Marketing Workbook for Women Who Want It All*, show women how to build a profitable network marketing business inside their sweet spot without sacrificing why they're doing it in the first place . . . even while running around with the kids. Kacie's second book, *The Sweet Spot: Everything Women Need to Know to Enjoy Life More*, gives women permission to enjoy life more. Whether you want a radical career change or just a little extra money for your family trip to Disney, Kacie can help you follow your passion. Create your intentional lifestyle at www.KacieVaudrey.com.

www.ingramcontent.com/pod-product-compliance
Lightning Source LLC
LaVergne TN
LVHW041223080426
835508LV00011B/1061